WOK COOKERY

HAMLYN

Published by The Hamlyn Publishing Group Limited,
part of Reed International Books,
Michelin House, 81 Fulham Road, London SW3 6RB

First published in this edition 1988

Additional photography by David Jordan

The publishers would like to thank G.F. Smith & Son,
London, Ltd. for permission to use their Parch Marque
papers as background colours in this book.

ISBN 0 600 55763 4

Typeset in Bembo by Servis Filmsetting Ltd, Manchester
Produced by Mandarin Offset
Printed and bound in Hong Kong

Contents

Introduction

An exciting feature of the thin, curved metal wok traditionally used for Chinese cooking is that it opens up the cuisine of much of Asia. Other oriental countries use similar pans with other names: in Korea, such a pan is called a *sot*, in Malaysia, Singapore and Indonesia a *wajan*, in India a *karahi*, in Burma a *dar-o* and in the Philippines a *carajay*.

The Wok

The traditional and most common type of wok is that made from carbon or tempered steel. Made of thin metal, a wok like this heats up very quickly and it is very responsive to an increase or decrease in heat. However, without care, this type of wok rusts easily – it needs to be kept oiled and free from damp but if used fairly frequently, it is the best type to buy. After extensive use the steel builds up an excellent cooking surface – blackened, and relatively non-stick. Make sure the lid is either of stainless steel or aluminium; a carbon steel lid presents a permanent rust problem and it can be a great nuisance! Look at the type of handles on the wok; some have a pair of metal handles – these will become very hot during cooking – while others have a pair of handles with wooden grips or a single wooden handle, both of which are quite practical.

When new, carbon steel woks have a wax coating which has to be removed by washing the wok in hot soapy water. The wok should be rinsed and thoroughly dried, then seasoned. To do this heat the wok and pour in a little oil, then rub it around the pan with a pad of absorbent kitchen paper. Heat the wok until it is smoking hot, wipe it again and repeat once more. Wipe the outside of the wok with oil too.

After cooking with fat, there is no need to wash the wok – it should be washed as rarely as possible – simply wipe it out with plenty of absorbent kitchen paper and use salt as a scouring agent, if necessary, with a little fresh oil to clean the surface. If you have prepared a saucy dish or one which has stuck slightly, then wash the wok in soapy water and re-season it. This type of wok is best kept hanging in a dry, well-ventilated place.

Stainless steel woks and those with a non-stick coating are also available, as well as non-stick and carbon steel electric woks. Follow the manufacturer's instructions for the care of these utensils.

Accessories

Most woks come complete with a metal stand to place over the cooker hob. These stands have sloping sides, which enable the wok to be held near to the heat source, as required in the case of an electric ring, or, when the stand is turned over, it keeps the wok above a gas flame. These stands can also be purchased separately.

Second only in importance to the stand is the lid. This is the accessory needed for braising and steaming in the wok. Make sure that the lid fits well and that it has a wooden knob or one which will not become too hot when in use. A steaming rack is also important for cooking in the wok and it is usually included in wok kits; if not, one can be bought separately.

Bamboo steamers are very useful because they can be rested in the wok and several layers can be stacked one on top of another, to cook or reheat a selection of dishes at the same time. If you are going to buy a set, choose those with a reasonably large diameter.

A variety of small accessories, such as ladles and spoons for tossing, turning, stirring and draining foods, is also available. These are not essential – if you have a reasonably well-equipped kitchen then you do not need them – but they do add to the fun of cooking in your wok.

A pestle and mortar, made of wood, stone, glass or porcelain are useful for pounding ingredients to a paste and for grinding and mixing spices.

COOKING METHODS

When there are several dishes to be prepared in the wok for one meal, cook those which take the longest first, and cook stir-fried foods at the last minute. Remember, some foods can be steamed over a dish braising in the well of the wok.

Stir-frying

This is the method most commonly associated with wok cooking and a traditional type of wok is by far the best appliance for this rapid food frying. The main advantage of the wok is its shape, which enables the heat to spread evenly so only a short cooking time is required. The hot, deep sides of the wok provide a large surface area and plenty of depth to sear and toss the food without throwing it out of the pan. It is most important to have all the ingredients ready before you start stir-frying and they should be cut evenly and finely.

The preparation of oriental food takes great care and often a longer time than the actual cooking. In Korea, China, Malaysia, Singapore and Indonesia, food is cut into small pieces and great importance is attached to the various methods of cutting. The result is that only a short cooking time is required and this helps to preserve the natural flavours. It is quite satisfying to practise and master these basic cutting skills.

Slicing The ingredients are cut into thin slices, normally not much larger than a postage stamp, and as thin as cardboard. When slicing meat, always cut across the grain, which makes the meat more tender when cooked. Vegetables, such as carrots, are often cut on the slant so that the slices have a larger surface area to absorb flavourings.

Shredding The ingredients are first sliced, then stacked like a pack of cards and cut into thin strips about the size of matchsticks.

Dicing The ingredients are first cut into strips as wide as they are thick, then cut at right angles to the same width to make cubes, usually about 1 cm/$\frac{1}{2}$ in.

Mincing The ingredients are very finely chopped in a mincer.

Diagonal cutting This method is normally used for cutting vegetables, such as carrots and celery. A diagonal cut is made straight down, then the vegetable is rolled a half-turn and sliced diagonally again, in order to obtain a diamond-shaped piece.

Shallow frying

You can use your wok for most of the shallow frying normally carried out in a frying pan. However it is sometimes better to use an ordinary frying pan – for example, several eggs cannot be fried together in the wok!

Deep frying

Because of its shape the wok is not ideal for deep frying loads of chips and it should not be used as a substitute for the western form of deep frying pan. However it is useful for frying small individual items of food, as the well of the wok gives a good depth of fat even if only a small amount is used.

Braising

The wok, with its domed lid, is ideal for braising foods, both large and small. The dish remains moist and quite large quantities can be cooked in this way – even whole birds can be braised in a wok.

Steaming

The wok makes a wonderful steamer. With the steaming rack in place, puddings, fish, meat and rice can be steamed. The domed lid allows plenty of room for the food dishes or basins to stand on the rack and it also helps the steam to condense quickly during cooking. For long steaming the water does have to be topped up, but for short steaming times sufficient moisture runs back down into the wok.

A glossary is provided at the back of the book (see page 62) describing ingredients which may be unfamiliar.

Soups

SHREDDED PORK AND NOODLE SOUP

SERVES 4

**3–4 dried Chinese mushrooms, soaked in
  warm water for 30 minutes
225 g/8 oz boned lean pork, shredded
1 tablespoon soy sauce
1 tablespoon rice wine or sherry
1 teaspoon sugar
2 teaspoons cornflour
350 g/2 oz egg noodles
3 tablespoons oil
2 spring onions, cut into 2.5-cm/1-in lengths
100 g/4 oz bamboo shoot, shredded
salt
600 ml/1 pint boiling chicken stock**

Drain the mushrooms, then squeeze dry, reserving
the soaking liquid. Discard the hard stalks, then
slice the caps into thin strips.

Put the pork in a bowl with the soy sauce, wine,
sugar and cornflour. Stir well, then leave to
marinate for about 20 minutes.

Cook the noodles in boiling water for about 5
minutes. Drain.

Heat half the oil in a wok and stir-fry the pork
until it changes colour. Remove from the wok
with a slotted spoon and drain.

Heat the remaining oil in the wok, add the
spring onions, then the mushrooms and bamboo
shoot. Stir, then add a little salt. Return the pork to
the wok together with the soaking liquid from the
mushrooms.

Place the noodles in a warmed large serving
bowl, pour over the boiling stock, then add the
pork and vegetables. Serve hot.

DUCK AND CABBAGE SOUP

SERVES 4

If a duck carcass is not available, use a duck portion
in this recipe. Fry the duck in 1–2 teaspoons oil in
the wok until cooked through. Discard skin and
cut meat off bone. Pour off oil from wok.
Continue recipe as below.

**1 duck carcass, with giblets
2 slices fresh root ginger, peeled
450 g/1 lb Chinese cabbage, sliced
salt and freshly ground black pepper**

Break up the carcass, then place in a wok. Add the
giblets and any other meat left over from the duck.

Cover with water, add the ginger, then bring to the boil and skim. Lower the heat and simmer gently for at least 30 minutes.

Add the cabbage and season to taste. Continue cooking for about 20 minutes.

Discard the duck carcass and ginger, taste and adjust the seasoning. Pour into a warmed soup tureen. Serve hot.

Variation

For Chicken and Cabbage Soup, use a chicken carcass and giblets and add a little grated lemon rind to enhance the flavour of the chicken.

CHINESE CAULIFLOWER SOUP

SERVES 4

1 small cauliflower, finely chopped
100 g/4 oz chicken meat, coarsely chopped
1 litre/1¾ pints chicken stock
2 eggs, beaten
1 teaspoon salt
50 g/2 oz lean ham, finely chopped
chopped fresh coriander to garnish

Put the cauliflower, chicken and stock in a wok and cook gently for 15–20 minutes.

Pour the eggs into the soup, then stir in the salt. Add the ham. Pour into a warmed soup tureen and sprinkle with coriander. Serve hot.

FISH SOUP WITH COCONUT

SERVES 4

350 g/12 oz desiccated coconut
750 ml/1¼ pints boiling water
575 g/1¼ lb monkfish or halibut fillet, skinned and cut into 2.5-cm/1-in cubes
salt
6 shallots or small onions
6 whole almonds, blanched
2–3 cloves garlic
2.5-cm/1-in piece fresh root ginger, peeled and sliced
2 stems lemon grass, trimmed and root discarded
2–3 teaspoons turmeric
3 tablespoons oil
1–3 fresh chillies, seeded and finely sliced
sprigs of parsley or coriander to garnish

To make coconut milk, put 300 g/11 oz of the desiccated coconut and the boiling water into a liquidiser or food processor and blend for 20 seconds. Pour into a bowl and cool to blood heat. Strain the milk into a clean bowl. Squeeze the coconut firmly over the sieve to obtain the coconut milk. When the coconut cream rises to the top of the coconut milk, spoon off 50 ml/2 fl oz and reserve.

Sprinkle the fish liberally with salt.

Place the remaining desiccated coconut in a wok and heat until golden and crisp, turning constantly to prevent burning. This will take several minutes. Blend or pound until the coconut appears oily, then transfer to a bowl and reserve.

Pound or blend the onions, almonds, garlic, ginger and 6 cm/2½ in from the root end of the lemon grass stems (reserve the remainder) in a pestle and mortar, liquidiser or food processor, to make a paste. Add the turmeric.

Heat the oil in the wok and fry the pounded mixture for a few minutes but do not allow to brown. Add the coconut milk, stirring constantly as it comes to the boil to prevent curdling.

Add the cubes of fish, most of the chilli and the stems of lemon grass and cook for 3–4 minutes. Stir in the pounded coconut, moistened with some of the soup if necessary and cook for a further 2–3 minutes. Do not overcook the fish.

Taste and adjust the seasoning and stir in the coconut cream just before serving. Remove the stems of lemon grass. Transfer to a warmed soup tureen and sprinkle with the remaining chilli. Garnish with parsley or coriander.

MULLIGATAWNY SOUP

SERVES 6

450 g/1 lb shin of beef, cut into 2.5-cm/1-in cubes
1 kg/2 lb beef bones, washed
about 2.25 litres/4 pints water
1 tablespoon coriander seeds
½ teaspoon black peppercorns
2 teaspoons cumin seeds
1 teaspoon turmeric
6 green cardamom pods, lightly bruised
2–3 whole cloves
4 cloves garlic, crushed
salt
2 potatoes, peeled and diced
1 tablespoon oil
1 large onion, finely sliced
1 teaspoon garam masala or 1 teaspoon mild curry powder
600 ml/1 pint coconut milk, using 225 g/8 oz desiccated coconut and 750 ml/1¼ pints boiling water (see this page)
juice of 1 lemon
few curry plant leaves or fresh coriander to garnish (optional)
croûtes of fried bread sprinkled with mustard or poppy seeds to serve

Place the beef and bones in a wok with the water. Add the coriander seeds, peppercorns, cumin, turmeric, cardamom, cloves and garlic with salt to taste. Bring to the boil and skim. Cover and simmer for about 2 hours until the meat is tender. Cool slightly.

Lift out the bones and discard. Remove the meat, shred finely and reserve. Strain the soup and remove the spices.

Return 1.75 litres/3 pints of the soup to the rinsed wok with the potato. Bring to the boil, cover and cook for 20 minutes until the potato is tender. Stir in the reserved meat and set the wok aside.

Heat the oil in another wok or large pan and fry the onion until just beginning to colour. Add the garam masala or curry powder. Remove from the heat and stir in the coconut milk.

Stir the milk mixture into the soup. Add the lemon juice and reheat without boiling to avoid curdling.

Garnish with curry leaves or coriander. Hand round croûtes of fried bread to serve.

Top: Fish Soup with Coconut; *bottom*: Mulligatawny Soup

Starters and Snacks

SPICED FRIED PRAWNS

SERVES 4

This dish should really be made with freshly boiled prawns, but it is still delicious with precooked prawns from the fishmonger. Serve as a side dish with rice, or as a snack.

450 g/1 lb cooked prawns
2 tablespoons tamarind water
pinch of turmeric
1 teaspoon grated fresh root ginger
2 shallots or ½ onion, sliced
2 cloves garlic, crushed
1 tablespoon light soy sauce
150 ml/¼ pint oil

Batter
scant 75 g/3 oz rice powder or plain flour
4 tablespoons water
salt and freshly ground black pepper
1 size 6/small egg, beaten

Discard the heads and shells from the prawns, but leave on the tails. Devein them. Place in a bowl with the tamarind water, turmeric, ginger, shallots, garlic and soy sauce. Stir well, then marinate for at least 30 minutes.

Meanwhile make the batter. Put the rice powder or flour in a bowl and gradually stir in the water. Add salt and pepper to taste, then gradually beat in the egg.

Drain the marinade from the prawns and shallots. Dip the prawns and shallots into the batter.

Heat the oil in a wok and add the prawns and shallots, one at a time, until the bottom of the wok is covered. Fry until golden brown and crisp, then turn over and fry the underside. Serve hot or cold.

PRAWNS AND EGGS IN SPICY COCONUT SAUCE

SERVES 4

King prawns have a fine flavour but they are expensive, instead you can use small peeled cooked prawns in which case you will not have to devein them.

575 g/1¼ lb cooked, peeled large or king prawns
5 macadamias, chopped
3 red chillies, seeded and chopped
1 small onion, chopped
2 cloves garlic, chopped
½ teaspoon dried shrimp paste
2 teaspoons ground coriander
1 teaspoon grated fresh root ginger
2 tablespoons oil
3 ripe tomatoes, peeled, seeded and chopped
salt
1 bay leaf
1 stalk lemon grass (optional)
150 ml/¼ pint water
150 ml/¼ pint thick coconut milk
4 hard-boiled eggs, halved
75 g/3 oz mange-tout peas, trimmed

Garnish
1 cooked large or king prawn, unpeeled
twist of lemon

Cut each prawn in half and devein.

Put the macadamias, chillies, onion, garlic, shrimp paste, coriander and ginger in a food processor and work to a very smooth paste.

Heat the oil in a wok and fry the spice paste for 1 minute, stirring constantly. Add the prawns, tomatoes and salt to taste. Stir, then cover and simmer gently for 2 minutes.

Stir in the bay leaf, lemon grass, if using, and water. Increase the heat and boil, uncovered, for 5 minutes.

Lower the heat, add the coconut milk and eggs and simmer for 8 minutes. Add the mange-tout peas and simmer for 3 minutes or until tender and the sauce is thick. Taste and adjust the seasoning, then transfer to a warmed serving dish and garnish with the prawn and lemon twist. Serve hot.

PRAWN AND BEAN SPROUT FRITTERS

SERVES 4 or 6–8 AS A SIDE DISH

100 g/4 oz cooked, peeled prawns, minced
225 g/8 oz bean sprouts
4 spring onions, thinly sliced
2 shallots or ½ small onion, finely sliced
2 cloves garlic, crushed
2 tablespoons chopped fresh coriander
2 teaspoons grated fresh root ginger
2 tablespoons grated fresh coconut (optional)
50 g/2 oz rice flour or self-raising flour
1 teaspoon baking powder
1 teaspoon ground coriander
½ teaspoon chilli powder
3 tablespoons water
1 egg, beaten · salt and pepper
oil for deep frying
slices of lemon to garnish

Put all the ingredients except the oil in a bowl and mix well. Form the mixture into small balls about the size of walnuts.

Heat the oil in a wok and fry the fritters for 1½–2 minutes until golden brown. Remove from the pan with a slotted spoon and drain on absorbent kitchen paper. Transfer to a serving dish and garnish with lemon slices. Serve hot or cold.

PAN-FRIED MEAT DUMPLINGS

SERVES 4

These are not the type of dumplings normally found in stews – they look rather like miniature Cornish pasties and are wrapped in a very thin dough which is available from Chinese supermarkets. The Koreans often pinch the wun tun skins decoratively, or pull the edges of the crescent down and twist them together to form a shape like a hat with a brim. Serve hot as part of a main meal, or cold as part of an hors d'oeuvre.

225 g/8 oz topside of beef, minced
$\frac{1}{2}$ teaspoon sesame seeds
1 teaspoon sesame oil
2 teaspoons chopped spring onion
1 teaspoon crushed garlic
$\frac{1}{2}$ teaspoon salt
30 wun tun skins
4 tablespoons oil

To serve
turnip (optional)
sprig of parsley (optional)
Korean Soy Sauce (see opposite)

Put all the ingredients in a bowl, except the wun tun skins and oil. Mix well, then put a small teaspoon of the mixture in the centre of each wun tun skin. Fold the skin over and pinch together to form a semi-circle or triangle.

Drop the dumplings into a pan of boiling water and boil for 3 minutes. Remove the dumplings from the water with a slotted spoon and drain well. Heat the oil in a wok and fry the dumplings until golden, turning constantly. Remove and drain.

Arrange on a serving dish. Garnish, if liked, with flower shapes, cut from turnip, and parsley. Serve hot or cold, with Korean soy sauce as a dip.

SAVOURY-COATED COURGETTES

SERVES 4

400 g/14 oz large courgettes, thinly sliced
salt
100 g/4 oz bean curd (optional)
100 g/4 oz topside of beef, minced
2 teaspoons sesame seeds
2 teaspoons sesame oil
1 tablespoon chopped spring onion
1 teaspoon crushed garlic
$\frac{1}{2}$ teaspoon freshly ground black pepper
100 g/4 oz plain flour
3 size 6/small eggs, beaten
4 tablespoons oil

To serve
carrot (optional)
sprig of parsley (optional)
Korean Soy Sauce (see opposite)

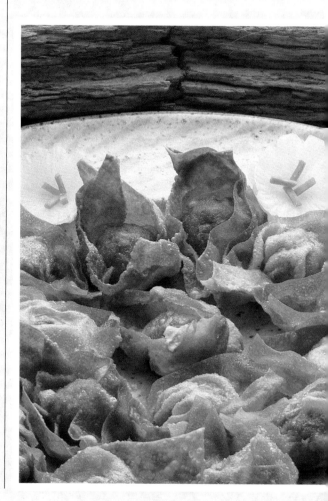

Put the courgettes in a single layer on a plate, sprinkle with salt, then set aside.

Mash the bean curd, then squeeze out the water until the bean curd is dry. Place in a bowl with the beef, sesame seeds, sesame oil, spring onions, garlic, pepper and salt to taste. Mix well.

Dip one side of each courgette slice in flour. Spread a little beef mixture on the floured side, pressing down well and spreading it out to cover. Dip both sides of each courgette slice in more flour, then in the egg.

Heat the oil in a wok, add the courgette slices, meat side down, and fry for 2–3 minutes until brown. Turn the slices over and fry until the underside is golden. Remove with a slotted spoon and drain on absorbent kitchen paper.

Arrange on a serving dish. Garnish, if liked, with flower shapes, cut from carrot, and parsley. Serve hot or cold, with Korean soy sauce handed separately as a dip.

KOREAN SOY SAUCE

SERVES 4

This is a basic soy sauce which is enhanced by additional ingredients. It is served in individual bowls as a dip.

3 tablespoons soy sauce
1 tablespoon chopped spring onion
1 teaspoon sesame seeds
1 teaspoon sesame oil
1 teaspoon crushed garlic
$\frac{1}{2}$ teaspoon sugar
1 teaspoon vinegar
pinch of chilli powder

Mix all the ingredients together. Divide equally between 4 individual shallow dishes or serve in one larger bowl.

VIETNAMESE CRAB ROLLS

MAKES 16 ROLLS

Not unlike the Chinese spring roll, pork and crab is one of the favourite Vietnamese fillings for this crisp delicacy. Serve with a bowl of Tangy Chilli Sauce (see page 15).

Fillings
50 g/2 oz cellophane noodles, soaked in water for 10 minutes
6 dried Chinese mushrooms, soaked in warm water for 30 minutes
1 tablespoon oil
450 g/1 lb lean minced pork
8–10 spring onions, finely chopped
350 g/12 oz crabmeat, canned or fresh
4 egg yolks, lightly beaten
1 teaspoon salt
½ teaspoon white pepper

Wrappers
4 eggs, beaten
16 dried rice papers
450 ml/¾ pint oil for deep frying
shredded spring onion to garnish

Drain the cellophane noodles, then cut them into 2.5-cm/1-in pieces. Remove the stalks from the Chinese mushrooms and slice the caps.

To make the filling, combine the noodles with the mushrooms. Heat the oil in a wok and add the pork, mashing it constantly with the back of a spoon to break up any lumps. Cook for about 2 minutes. Remove from the heat and add the chopped spring onions, crabmeat, noodles and mushrooms, stirring constantly, then the egg yolks and seasoning. Mix well. Divide into 16 portions and pat each into the shape of a cylinder, about a finger's length.

To assemble each crab roll, brush the beaten egg over the entire surface of each piece of rice paper. Leave a few seconds until soft and flexible. Place the filling diagonally across the wrapper, roll over once, fold over the sides and roll once. Brush the exposed wrapper with beaten egg and roll into a neat package. (The beaten egg will seal the wrapper and keep the roll intact.) Place the crab rolls on a plate. Refrigerate the rolls, covered with cling film if liked, until ready to fry.

Heat the oil in a wok and deep fry the crab rolls, 3 or 4 at a time, turning them with a slotted spoon, for about 4–5 minutes or until golden brown and crispy. Drain on absorbent kitchen paper and keep warm while frying the remaining rolls. Serve the crab rolls hot, garnished with a few shredded spring onions.

CHICKEN SPRING ROLLS

MAKES 20 ROLLS

Spring rolls are the most popular dish in Vietnamese cuisine, for both rich and poor. They are usually filled with pork and crab, but a combination of any meat or seafood may be used. Serve as an appetizer with a bowl of Tangy Chilli Sauce (this page) or as a main course accompanied by a green salad with the sauce served separately in individual bowls as a dip.

Cooked spring rolls can be frozen, then reheated in a moderate oven (180 c/350 f, gas 4). Alternatively, they can be partially cooked, refrigerated for 1 day, then the cooking completed the following day.

Fillings
50 g/2 oz cellophane noodles, soaked in water for 10 minutes
2 tablespoons dried Chinese mushrooms, soaked in warm water for 30 minutes
450 g/1 lb chicken breast meat, skinned and cut into thin strips
3 cloves garlic, finely chopped
3 shallots, finely chopped
225 g/8 oz crabmeat, canned or frozen
½ teaspoon freshly ground black pepper

Wrappers
4 eggs, beaten
20 dried rice papers
450 ml/¾ pint oil for deep frying
shredded spring onion to garnish

Drain the cellophane noodles, then cut into 2.5-cm/1-in pieces. Finely chop the mushrooms.

To make the filling, put all the ingredients in a bowl and mix well by hand. Divide the mixture into 20 portions and shape into small cylinders.

To assemble each spring roll, brush beaten egg over the entire surface of each piece of rice paper. Leave for a few seconds until soft and flexible. Place the prepared filling along the curved edge of the paper, roll once, then fold over the sides to enclose the filling and continue rolling. (The beaten egg holds the wrapper together.)

Heat the oil in a wok and deep fry about one-third of the spring rolls over moderate heat until golden brown. Remove with a slotted spoon and drain on absorbent kitchen paper. Fry the remaining spring rolls in the same way. Serve hot or at room temperature, garnished with shredded spring onion.

TANGY CHILLI SAUCE

SERVES 4

This Vietnamese hot, tangy sauce is sprinkled on food as desired and incorporated into many recipes. Tangy Chilli Sauce can be made in larger quantities and stored in the refrigerator for up to 1 week. Keep in a small glass jar with a tightly-fitting lid.

2 cloves garlic
4 dried red chillies or 1 fresh red chilli
5 teaspoons sugar
juice and pulp of ¼ lime
4 tablespoons fish sauce
5 tablespoons water

Pound the garlic, chillies and sugar using a pestle and mortar. Alternatively, place the ingredients in a bowl and mash with the back of a spoon.

Add the lime juice and pulp, then the fish sauce and water. Mix well to combine the ingredients. Use as required.

Seafood

STIR-FRIED SQUID WITH MIXED VEGETABLES

SERVES 4

Do not overcook the squid or it will be tough and chewy. When buying, remember squid are at their tenderest when small.

400 g/14 oz squid
2 slices fresh root ginger, peeled and finely chopped
1 tablespoon rice wine or sherry
1 tablespoon cornflour
15 g/½ oz dried Chinese mushrooms, soaked in warm water for 30 minutes
4 tablespoons oil
2 spring onions, cut into 2.5-cm/1-in lengths
225 g/8 oz cauliflower or broccoli, divided into florets
2 medium carrots, cut into diamond-shaped chunks
1 teaspoon salt
1 teaspoon sugar
1 teaspoon sesame oil

Clean the squid, discarding the head, transparent backbone and ink bag. Cut the flesh into thin slices or rings. Place in a bowl with half the ginger, the wine and cornflour. Mix well, then leave to marinate for about 20 minutes.

Meanwhile, drain the Chinese mushrooms and break into small pieces, discarding the hard pieces.

Heat 2 tablespoons of the oil in a wok and add the spring onions and remaining ginger, then the cauliflower or broccoli, carrots and Chinese mushrooms. Stir-fry, then add the salt and sugar and continue cooking until the vegetables are tender, adding a little water if necessary. Remove the vegetables from the wok with a slotted spoon and drain.

Heat the remaining oil in the wok and stir-fry the squid for about 1 minute. Return the vegetables to the wok, add the sesame oil and mix all the ingredients well together. Serve hot.

CRAB OMELETTE

SERVES 3–4

2 spring onions
4 eggs, beaten
salt
3 tablespoons oil
2 slices fresh root ginger, peeled and shredded
175 g/6 oz crabmeat, fresh, frozen or canned
1 tablespoon rice wine or sherry
1 tablespoon soy sauce
2 teaspoons sugar

Garnish
shredded lettuce
serrated-cut tomato half (optional)
grape (optional)

Cut white part of the spring onions into 2.5-cm/1-in lengths. Chop the green part finely and beat into the eggs, with salt to taste.

Heat the oil in a wok and add the white part of the spring onions and the ginger, then the crab and wine. Stir-fry for a few seconds, then add the soy sauce and sugar.

Lower the heat, pour in the egg mixture and cook for a further 30 seconds.

Transfer to a warmed serving plate and garnish with shredded lettuce. To finish, place a tomato half and a grape in the centre to resemble a flower head, if liked. Serve immediately.

Top: Stir-fried Squid with Mixed Vegetables; *bottom:* Crab Omelette

MILD CRAB CURRY

SERVES 4

A mild curry, using crabmeat, which is a popular ingredient for curries from the coastal areas of India. If using frozen crabmeat, it should be allowed to thaw completely.

2–3 tablespoons oil
1 medium onion, finely chopped
1 clove garlic, crushed
1 tablespoon chopped fresh coriander
1 teaspoon grated nutmeg
1 teaspoon chilli powder
1 teaspoon sugar
salt
1 (400-g/14-oz) can tomatoes, chopped with
    the juice
450 g/1 lb cooked crabmeat, fresh, canned or
    frozen

Heat the oil in a wok and fry the onion until just soft and transparent. Add the garlic, coriander, nutmeg, chilli, sugar and salt. Stir and cook for a further 2–3 minutes. Add the tomatoes and cook gently for 25–30 minutes until reduced to a thick sauce.

Using a fork, break the crabmeat into small chunks and gently stir into the sauce. Cover and simmer very gently for 5–7 minutes. Serve with plain boiled rice, Sweetcorn Curry (page 56), a green salad, poppadums, chutneys and pickles.

STIR-FRIED PRAWNS AND PEPPER

SERVES 4

2–3 tablespoons oil
1 large onion, finely chopped
2 tablespoons ground coriander
50 g/2 oz desiccated coconut
450 g/1 lb cooked, peeled prawns, thawed if
  frozen
1 teaspoon salt
1 teaspoon chilli powder
¼ teaspoon turmeric
1 large green pepper, seeded and diced

Heat the oil in a wok and fry the onion until just soft and transparent. Add the coriander and coconut and fry for 2 minutes. Add the prawns and stir-fry for about 5 minutes until they are thoroughly heated through.

Finally, add the salt, chilli powder, turmeric and green pepper and stir-fry for a further 2–3 minutes. Serve immediately, accompanied by plain boiled rice.

Note: A firm textured white fish such as monkfish or halibut, cut into small pieces may be substituted for some of the prawns in this dish, but add it before the prawns and stir-fry for 4–5 minutes before continuing with the recipe.

PRAWN BALLS WITH BROCCOLI

SERVES 4

Do not overcook the prawns or they will lose their delicate flavour.

225 g/8 oz large or king prawns, unshelled, heads removed
1 slice fresh root ginger, peeled and finely chopped
1 teaspoon rice wine or sherry
1 egg white
1 tablespoon cornflour
3 tablespoons oil
2 spring onions, finely chopped
225 g/8 oz broccoli, cut into small pieces
1 teaspoon salt
1 teaspoon sugar

Wash and peel the prawns and dry thoroughly with absorbent kitchen paper. Use a sharp knife to make a shallow incision down the back of the prawn and pull out the black intestinal vein. Split each prawn in half lengthways, then cut into small pieces so that they become little round balls when cooked.

Put the prawns in a bowl with the ginger, wine, egg white and cornflour. Stir well, then leave to marinate in the refrigerator for about 20 minutes.

Heat 1 tablespoon of the oil in a wok and stir-fry the prawns over moderate heat until they change colour. Remove from the wok with a slotted spoon.

Heat the remaining oil in the wok, add the spring onions and broccoli, stir, then add the salt and sugar. Cook until the broccoli is just tender. Return the prawns to the wok and stir well to combine the ingredients thoroughly. Serve hot.

RED SNAPPER WITH SWEET AND SOUR SAUCE

SERVES 4–6

15 g/½ oz dried Chinese mushrooms, soaked in warm water for 30 minutes
1 (675g–1-kg/1½–2-lb) red snapper, grey mullet, or other whole fish
2 teaspoons salt
3 tablespoons flour
4 tablespoons oil
2–3 spring onions, shredded
2 slices fresh root ginger, peeled and shredded
1 clove garlic, finely chopped
15 g/½ oz bamboo shoot, thinly sliced
50 g/2 oz water chestnuts, thinly sliced
1 red pepper, seeded and shredded
3 tablespoons wine vinegar

Sauce
3 tablespoons sugar
2 tablespoons soy sauce
2 tablespoons rice wine or sherry
2 teaspoons cornflour
150 ml/¼ pint chicken stock or water
1 teaspoon chilli sauce

Drain the Chinese mushrooms and slice very thinly, discarding the hard pieces.

Clean the fish thoroughly and remove the fins and tail but leave the head on. Make diagonal slashes through to the bone along both sides of the fish at 5-mm/¼-in intervals. Dry thoroughly, then rub the fish inside and out with 1 teaspoon of the salt. Coat with the flour from head to tail.

Heat the oil in a wok until very hot. Lower the heat a little, add the fish and fry for about 4–5 minutes on each side until golden and crisp, turning the fish carefully. Drain, then transfer carefully to a warmed serving dish. Keep hot.

Add the spring onions, ginger and garlic to the oil remaining in the wok. Stir in the Chinese mushrooms, bamboo shoot, water chestnuts and red pepper, then the remaining salt and the vinegar.

Mix the sauce ingredients together and add to the wok. Cook, stirring, until thickened. Pour the sweet and sour sauce over the fish and serve immediately.

Top: Red Snapper with Sweet and Sour Sauce; *bottom*: Prawn Balls with Broccoli

Chicken and Pork Dishes

FOIL-WRAPPED CHICKEN

SERVES 4

This is a variation of the traditional Chinese recipe, paper-wrapped chicken. Prawns or other meat can be used instead of chicken.

450 g/1 lb skinned chicken breast meat
3 spring onions, white part only
¼ teaspoon salt
1 tablespoon soy sauce
1 teaspoon sugar
1 teaspoon rice wine or sherry
1 teaspoon sesame oil
4 tablespoons oil

Garnish
shredded spring onion
finely chopped red pepper

Cut the chicken into 12 roughly equal-sized pieces. Cut each spring onion ino 4 pieces. Combine the chicken and spring onions with the salt, soy sauce, sugar, wine and sesame oil in a bowl. Leave to marinate for about 20 minutes.

Cut 12 squares of foil large enough to wrap around the chicken pieces four times. Brush the pieces of foil with oil, then place a piece of chicken on each. Top with a piece of spring onion, then wrap the foil around the chicken to make a parcel, completely enclosing it.

Heat the oil in a wok and fry the chicken parcels over moderate heat for about 2 minutes on each side. Remove and leave to drain on a wok rack for a few minutes; turn off the heat.

Reheat the oil. When very hot, return the chicken parcels to the wok and fry for 1 minute only. Serve hot in the foil, garnished with shredded spring onion and red pepper.

LOTUS-WHITE CHICKEN

SERVES 4

5 egg whites
120 ml/4 fl oz chicken stock
1 teaspoon salt
1 teaspoon rice wine or sherry
2 teaspoons cornflour
100 g/4 oz chicken breast meat, skinned and finely chopped
oil for deep frying

Garnish
1–2 tablespoons cooked peas
25 g/1 oz cooked ham, shredded

Put the egg whites in a bowl. Stir in 3 tablespoons of the chicken stock, the salt, wine and half the cornflour. Add the chicken and mix well.

Heat the oil in a wok to 180c/350f. Gently pour in about one-third of the egg and chicken mixture. Deep fry for 10 seconds until the mixture

begins to rise to the surface, then carefully turn over. Deep fry until golden. Remove from the wok with a slotted spoon, drain and place on a warmed serving dish. Keep hot while cooking the remainder.

Heat the remaining stock in a small pan. Mix the remaining cornflour to a paste with a little cold water, add to the stock and simmer, stirring, until thickened. Pour over the chicken. Garnish with the peas and ham. Serve hot.

Clockwise from top right: Fried Chicken Legs; Foil-wrapped Chicken; Lotus-white Chicken

FRIED CHICKEN LEGS

SERVES 4

6 chicken leg portions
2 tablespoons soy sauce
1 tablespoon rice wine or sherry
$\frac{1}{2}$ teaspoon freshly ground black pepper
2 tablespoons cornflour
300 ml/$\frac{1}{2}$ pint oil for deep frying
1 tablespoon finely chopped spring onion

Chop each chicken leg into 2 or 3 pieces. Mix with the soy sauce, wine and pepper in a bowl. Leave to marinate for about 20 minutes, turning occasionally.

Coat each piece of chicken with cornflour. Heat the oil in a wok to 180 c/350 f. Lower the heat and deep fry the chicken pieces until golden. Remove from the wok with a slotted spoon and drain.

Pour off all but 1 tablespoon oil, then add the spring onion to the wok with the drained chicken pieces. Stir-fry over moderate heat for about 2 minutes. Serve hot.

GINGER CHICKEN

SERVES 4

4 chicken breasts, about 675 g/1½ lb, boned
    and cut into finger-sized pieces
1 teaspoon sugar
salt and freshly ground black pepper
7.5–10 cm/3–4-in piece fresh root ginger,
    peeled and finely sliced
4 tablespoons sesame oil
75–120 ml/3–4 fl oz water
100 g/4 oz button mushrooms
2 tablespoons brandy
2 teaspoons cornflour, blended with
    3 tablespoons water
1 teaspoon soy sauce
fresh coriander leaves to garnish

Sprinkle the chicken with the sugar and leave to
stand for 20–30 minutes, this helps to release the
juices. Add the salt and pepper.

Heat the oil in a wok and fry the ginger slices.
Add the chicken pieces and cook for 3 minutes.
Stir in the water and mushrooms. Cover and cook
for a further 5 minutes, or until the chicken is
tender.

Add the brandy, blended cornflour and soy
sauce. Bring to the boil, stirring constantly until
the sauce thickens. Taste and adjust the seasoning.
Arrange on a warmed serving plate and garnish
with the coriander leaves.

Top: Chilli Chicken; *bottom*: Ginger Chicken

CHILLI CHICKEN

SERVES 4

It is important to use red not green chillies for their
colour.

4 chicken breasts, about 675 g/1½ lb, boned and
    skinned
1 teaspoon sugar
3–6 fresh red chillies, seeded if preferred
2 macadamia nuts or 4 almonds
1 stem lemon grass, trimmed and sliced
1 teaspoon fenugreek
2.5-cm/1-in piece fresh root ginger, peeled
6 small red onions or shallots, sliced
4 cloves garlic, crushed
4 tablespoons oil
150 ml/¼ pint water
salt
shredded spring onion to garnish

Cut each chicken breast lengthways into 8 pieces
and sprinkle with the sugar.

Pound the chillies with the nuts, lemon grass,
fenugreek and half the ginger in a pestle and
mortar or blend in a food processor or liquidiser.
Transfer to a small bowl. Pound or blend the
remaining ginger with the onions and garlic in the
same way.

Heat the oil in a wok and fry the spice mixture
for 1–2 minutes. Add the onion mixture and fry
for a further 1–2 minutes, stirring constantly.

Add the chicken pieces, turning in the sauce
until well coated. Add the water and salt to taste.
Cover and cook gently for 5 minutes. Transfer to a
warmed serving dish and garnish with spring
onion.

BRAISED CHICKEN WINGS

SERVES 4

12 chicken wings
4 dried Chinese mushrooms, soaked in warm
  water for 30 minutes
2 tablespoons oil
2 spring onions, finely chopped
2 slices fresh root ginger, peeled and finely
  chopped
2 tablespoons soy sauce
2 tablespoons rice wine or sherry
1 tablespoon sugar
$\frac{1}{2}$ teaspoon five-spice powder
350 ml/12 fl oz water
175 g/6 oz bamboo shoot, cut into chunks
2 teaspoons cornflour, blended with a little
  water

Trim and discard the tips of the chicken wings, then cut each wing into 2 pieces by breaking the joint.

Squeeze the mushrooms dry, discard the stalks, then cut the caps into small pieces.

Heat the oil in a wok until it reaches smoking point. Add the spring onions and ginger, then the chicken wings. Stir-fry until the chicken changes colour, then add the soy sauce, wine, sugar, five-spice powder and water.

Lower the heat and cook gently until the liquid has reduced by about half. Add the mushrooms and bamboo shoot and continue cooking until the juice has almost completely evaporated. Remove the bamboo shoot chunks, rinse, drain and arrange them around the edge of a warmed serving dish.

Add the blended cornflour to the wok and cook, stirring constantly, until thickened. Place the chicken mixture on the centre of the bamboo shoot. Serve hot.

CHICKEN WINGS AND BROCCOLI ASSEMBLY

SERVES 4

12 chicken wings
4 spring onions, finely chopped
2 slices fresh root ginger, finely chopped
1 tablespoon lemon juice
1 tablespoon soy sauce
1½ teaspoons salt
1 tablespoon rice wine or dry sherry
4 tablespoons oil
225 g/8 oz broccoli, divided into florets
50 g/2 oz tomatoes, chopped
1 tablespoon cornflour, blended with a little
 water

Discard the tips of the chicken wings, then cut each wing into 2 pieces by breaking the joint.

Put the chicken in a bowl with the spring onions, ginger, lemon juice, soy sauce, ½ teaspoon of the salt and the wine. Stir well, then leave to marinate for about 20 minutes.

Heat 2 tablespoons of the oil in a wok and stir-fry the broccoli with the remaining salt until tender but still crisp. Arrange the broccoli neatly around the edge of a warmed serving dish and keep hot.

Remove the chicken pieces, reserving the marinade. Heat the remaining oil in the wok and fry the chicken until golden. Remove from the wok with a slotted spoon and drain.

Add the tomatoes to the wok and stir-fry until reduced to a pulp. Return the chicken to the wok and add the marinade. Cook for about 2 minutes, then add the blended cornflour and cook, stirring constantly, until thickened.

Spoon into the centre of the serving dish. Serve immediately.

THAI CHICKEN GINGER WITH HONEY

SERVES 4

The flavour of this dish is greatly improved if it is cooked the day before it is required, then reheated just before serving.

5 spring onions, cut into 1-cm/½-in pieces
50 g/2 oz fresh root ginger, shredded
2 tablespoons oil
3 chicken breasts, skinned, boned and
   cut into small pieces
3 chicken livers, chopped
1 onion, sliced
3 cloves garlic, chopped
2 tablespoons dried Chinese mushrooms,
   soaked in warm water for 30 minutes
2 tablespoons soy sauce
1 tablespoon honey

Put the spring onions in a bowl, cover with cold water and leave to soak.

Mix the ginger with a little cold water, then drain and squeeze to reduce the hot taste. Rinse under cold running water, then drain well.

Heat the oil in a wok and stir-fry the chicken and liver pieces for 5 minutes. Remove from the wok with a slotted spoon and set aside.

Add the onion to the wok and fry gently until soft, then add the garlic and mushrooms and stir-fry for 1 minute. Return the chicken pieces to the wok.

Mix the soy sauce and honey together, pour over the chicken and stir well. Add the ginger and stir-fry for 2–3 minutes, then add the drained spring onions.

Transfer the mixture to a bowl, cover and leave overnight. Reheat when required. Serve hot.

THAI FRIED PORK BALLS

SERVES 4

2 coriander roots, finely chopped
2 teaspoons freshly ground black pepper
4 cloves garlic
pinch of sugar
450 g/1 lb minced pork
2 tablespoons fish sauce
flour for coating
4–5 tablespoons oil
fresh coriander leaves to garnish

Put the coriander roots, pepper, garlic and sugar in a mortar or liquidiser and work to a smooth paste. Add the pork and pound to a pulp.

Transfer the mixture to a bowl and add the fish sauce. Stir well. Form the mixture into about 20 balls, approximately 2.5-cm/1-in in diameter, and coat lightly with flour.

Heat the oil in a wok and add about 5 pork balls. Fry over moderate heat for 2–3 minutes, or until no liquid is released from the balls when pierced with a sharp knife. Remove from the wok; keep hot while frying the rest.

Pile the pork balls in a warmed serving dish and garnish with the coriander. Serve hot.

Top: Thai Chicken Ginger with Honey; *bottom*: Fried Pork Balls

STIR-FRIED CHICKEN WITH GINGER

SERVES 4

2.5-cm/1-in piece fresh root ginger,
   peeled and shredded
salt
2 tablespoons oil
2 cloves garlic, chopped
6 chicken thighs, chopped into
   2.5-cm/1-in squares
1 tablespoon fish sauce
1 teaspoon sugar
1 tablespoon water
2 spring onions, cut into 5-cm/2-in pieces
coriander leaves or sprigs of parsley to
   garnish

Sprinkle the ginger with a little salt, leave to stand
for a few minutes, then squeeze and discard the
liquid. Rinse the ginger with water and squeeze
out the liquid again.

Heat the oil in a wok and stir-fry the garlic until
lightly browned. Add the ginger and stir-fry for 1
minute, then add the chicken. Stir in the remaining ingredients, except the spring onions, then
cover and cook over moderate heat for 10
minutes, or until the chicken is completely
cooked. Stir in the spring onions.

Transfer to a warmed serving dish and garnish
with coriander leaves or parsley sprigs.

Note: Fresh root ginger may be stored in a plastic
bag in the refrigerator for several weeks but check
to make sure that any cut ends do not develop a
mould. Turn to the Glossary starting on page 62
for further information about this piquant spice,
now widely available.

FRIED PORK SPARERIBS

SERVES 4

900 g/2 lb pork spareribs, cut into
   separate pieces
2 tablespoons fish sauce
1 tablespoon sugar
3 cloves garlic, chopped
pinch of freshly ground black pepper
3 tablespoons oil

Garnish (optional)
thinly pared strip of red chilli
sprig of parsley

Put the spareribs in a bowl, cover with the remaining ingredients except the oil. Leave to marinate for 30 minutes.

Heat the oil in a wok and gently fry the spareribs for about 10 minutes on each side until golden brown and cooked through.

Drain the spareribs and arrange on a warmed serving dish. Garnish with chilli and parsley, if liked, arranged to resemble a flower head.

STIR-FRIED PORK WITH BAMBOO SHOOT

SERVES 3–4

225 g/8 oz boned lean pork, thinly sliced
2 teaspoons rice wine or sherry
2 tablespoons soy sauce
3 tablespoons oil
1 clove garlic, chopped
275 g/10 oz bamboo shoot, thinly sliced
2 teaspoons vinegar

Garnish
shredded spring onion
tomato

Put the pork in a bowl with the wine and 2 teaspoons of the soy sauce. Mix well, then leave to marinate for about 20 minutes.

Heat the oil in a wok and fry the garlic until golden brown. Remove from the wok with a slotted spoon and discard.

Add the pork to the wok and stir-fry until it changes colour. Add the bamboo shoot, the remaining soy sauce and the vinegar. Stir-fry for about 30 seconds. Serve hot, garnished with shredded spring onion and tomato.

CHINESE SPICED PORK

SERVES 4

This is a Malaysian recipe but it was developed by the Chinese immigrants who influenced a great many recipes now popular in Indonesia and other parts of the Far East.

450 g/1 lb lean pork
6–8 shallots or 1 onion, chopped
6 dried red chillies, soaked
1 teaspoon dried shrimp paste
1 tablespoon water
2 tablespoons oil

3 tablespoons tamarind water
1 teaspoon sugar
½ teaspoon salt
250 ml/8 fl oz water

Cut the pork into short finger-length strips. Put the shallots, chillies, shrimp paste and water in a liquidiser and work to a paste.

Heat the oil in a wok and gently fry the paste, stirring, for 3–4 minutes. Add the pork strips and stir-fry until they change colour.

Add the remaining ingredients and simmer, uncovered, for about 45 minutes, stirring frequently until the meat is tender and the sauce has reduced and thickened.

INDONESIAN CHICKEN WITH SHRIMP SAUCE

SERVES 4

A spicy, rich chicken curry in a shrimp coconut sauce. Serve with rice and a few fresh sambals.

1.5 kg/3 lb chicken breast and thigh joints
1 onion, quartered
4 cloves garlic
2.5 cm/1-in piece fresh root ginger, peeled
  and chopped
3 red chillies, seeded and quartered
1 tablespoon water
3 tablespoons oil
1 teaspoon turmeric
1 teaspoon freshly ground black pepper
½ teaspoon dried shrimp paste
1 stem lemon grass or 2 strips lemon rind
2 teaspoons Chinese shrimp sauce, or fish sauce
1½ teaspoons salt
350 ml/12 fl oz coconut milk (see page 9)
1 tablespoon palm or raw sugar
2 tablespoons lime or lemon juice

Cut the chicken into pieces approximately 4-cm/1½-in. Put the onion, garlic, ginger and chillies with the water in a liquidiser and work until well chopped, almost a paste.

Heat the oil in a wok and gently fry the onion mixture, stirring, for about 3–4 minutes. Add the turmeric, pepper and shrimp paste and cook a minute longer. Add the lemon grass, shrimp sauce, salt and chicken pieces and stir-fry over medium heat until the chicken is well coated and starting to brown.

Add the coconut milk and sugar and bring slowly to the simmer. Cover and cook over a gentle heat for about 30 minutes until the chicken is tender and the gravy has thickened.

If the gravy is not thick enough, remove the chicken and keep warm. Reduce the gravy over a high heat, stirring constantly until reduced a little and thickened. Add the lime juice and spoon over the chicken.

Note: Tamarind water is obtained from the dried pulp of the acid-flavoured tamarind fruit, resembling a bean pod. The dried pulp is sold in blocks in oriental stores. Soak about 15 g/½ oz tamarind pulp in 150 ml/¼ pint water for 5–10 minutes, then squeeze, strain and use the water. Lime or lemon juice, or vinegar, may be used as a substitute but the subtle flavour of this recipe will not be the same.

PORK SLICES WITH CAULIFLOWER

SERVES 4

4 dried Chinese mushrooms, soaked in
   warm water for 30 minutes
225 g/8 oz boned lean pork, sliced
2 tablespoons soy sauce
1 tablespoon rice wine or sherry
1 tablespoon cornflour
1 medium cauliflower, divided into florets
salt
3 tablespoons oil
2 spring onions, cut into 2.5-cm/1-in lengths
1 slice fresh root ginger, peeled and cut
   into strips

Squeeze the mushrooms dry, discard the stalks, then cut the mushroom caps into halves or quarters, according to size.

Put the pork in a bowl and sprinkle with the soy sauce, wine and 1 teaspoon of the cornflour. Mix well, then leave to marinate for about 20 minutes.

Meanwhile, blanch the cauliflower in a pan of boiling salted water for 1–2 minutes, then drain and set aside.

Heat the oil in a wok and add the spring onions and ginger, then the pork. Stir-fry until the pork changes colour, then add the mushrooms and 1 teaspoon salt. Stir-fry for a further 1 minute, then add the cauliflower and stir well.

Mix the remaining cornflour to a paste with a little water, add to the wok and cook, stirring, until thickened.

Arrange the cauliflower around the edge of a warmed serving dish and pile the pork mixture into the centre. Serve hot.

BEAN SPROUTS WITH SHREDDED PORK

SERVES 4

225 g/8 oz fresh bean sprouts
350 g/12 oz boned lean pork, shredded
2 tablespoons soy sauce
2 teaspoons rice wine or sherry
2 teaspoons cornflour
3 tablespoons oil
2 spring onions, shredded
1 slice fresh root ginger, peeled and shredded
1 teaspoon salt
50 g/2 oz leeks, shredded

Rinse the bean sprouts in cold water, discarding any husks that float to the surface, then trim.

Put the pork in a bowl. Sprinkle with the soy sauce, wine and cornflour. Mix well, then leave to marinate for about 20 minutes.

Heat 1 tablespoon of the oil in a wok and add the spring onions and ginger, then the pork. Stir-fry until the pork changes colour, then remove the pork from the wok with a slotted spoon and drain.

Heat the remaining oil in the wok and add the salt, then the bean sprouts and leeks. Stir-fry for about 1 minute. Return the pork to the wok, stir well and cook for a further 1 minute. Serve hot.

STIR-FRIED PORK WITH EGG

SERVES 4

On a Chinese menu this dish would be called Mu-Hsu Pork. Mu-Hsu is the Chinese for laurel, which has bright yellow fragrant flowers in autumn. The dish owes its name to the bright yellow colour of the scrambled eggs which are mixed with the pork.

25 g/1 oz dried Chinese mushrooms, soaked in
    warm water for 30 minutes
4 spring onions, trimmed
225 g/8 oz pork fillet
4 eggs
salt
3 tablespoons vegetable oil
1 tablespoon soy sauce
2 teaspoons rice wine or sherry
1 teaspoon sesame seed oil

Drain the mushrooms and shred finely. Shred the spring onions. Cut the pork fillet into thin strips.

Beat the eggs with a little salt. Heat 1 tablespoon of the vegetable oil in a wok. Add the eggs and scramble lightly, removing them from the pan before they set too hard.

Heat the remaining vegetable oil in the wok, add the shredded spring onions and pork strips and stir-fry until the pork changes colour.

Add the shredded mushroom, salt to taste, the soy sauce and the wine. Stir-fry for about 2 minutes, then add the scrambled eggs and sesame seed oil.

Mix all the ingredients together and serve hot.

AUBERGINE AND PORK IN HOT SAUCE

SERVES 4

175 g/6 oz boned lean pork, shredded
2 spring onions, finely chopped
1 slice fresh root ginger, peeled and finely
  chopped
1 clove garlic, finely chopped
1 tablespoon soy sauce
2 teaspoons rice wine or sherry
1½ teaspoons cornflour
300 ml/½ pint oil for deep frying
225 g/8 oz aubergine, cut into diamond-
  shaped chunks
1 tablespoon chilli sauce
3–4 tablespoons chicken stock or water
chopped spring onion to garnish

Put the pork in a bowl with the spring onion, ginger, garlic, soy sauce, wine and cornflour. Mix well, then leave to marinate for about 20 minutes.

Heat the oil in a wok to 180 c/350 f. Lower the heat, add the aubergine and deep fry for about 1½ minutes. Remove from the wok with a slotted spoon and drain.

Pour off all but 1 tablespoon oil from the wok. Add the pork and stir-fry for about 1 minute. Add the aubergine and chilli sauce and cook for about 1½ minutes, then moisten with the stock or water. Simmer until the liquid has almost completely evaporated. Serve hot, garnished with chopped spring onion.

STIR-FRIED LIVER WITH SPINACH

SERVES 4

Avoid overcooking the pig's liver or it will become tough.

350 g/12 oz pig's liver, cut into thin triangular slices
2 tablespoons cornflour
4 tablespoons oil
450 g/1 lb fresh spinach leaves, washed and drained thoroughly
1 teaspoon salt
2 slices fresh root ginger, peeled
1 tablespoon soy sauce
1 tablespoon rice wine or sherry
shredded spring onion to garnish

Blanch the liver for a few seconds in boiling water. Drain and coat the slices with the cornflour.

Heat 2 tablespoons of the oil in a wok and stir-fry the spinach and salt for 2 minutes. Remove from the wok, then arrange around the edge of a warmed serving dish and keep hot.

Heat the remaining oil in the wok until it is very hot. Add the ginger, liver, soy sauce and wine. Stir well, then pour over the spinach. Serve immediately, garnished with shredded spring onion.

Beef and Lamb Dishes

STIR-FRIED BEEF WITH BROCCOLI

SERVES 4

225 g/8 oz lean rump steak, thinly sliced
2 teaspoons salt
2 teaspoons rice wine or sherry
1 tablespoon cornflour
4 tablespoons oil
225 g/8 oz broccoli, divided into small florets
little chicken stock or water (optional)
2 spring onions, cut into 2.5-cm/1-in lengths
100 g/4 oz button mushrooms, sliced
1 tablespoon soy sauce

Cut the beef into narrow strips. Put in a bowl with
½ teaspoon of the salt, the wine and cornflour and
mix well. Leave to marinate for 20 minutes.

Heat 2 tablespoons of the oil in a wok and stir-
fry the broccoli with the remaining salt for a few
minutes, adding a little stock or water to moisten if
necessary. Remove from the wok with a slotted
spoon and drain.

Heat the remaining oil in the wok and fry the
spring onions for a few seconds. Add the beef and
stir-fry until evenly browned. Stir in the mushrooms, soy sauce and broccoli. Heat through and
serve hot.

BEEF AND CARROT STEW

SERVES 4–6

2 tablespoons oil
1 clove garlic, crushed
1 slice fresh root ginger, peeled and chopped
1 spring onion, chopped
675 g/1½ lb stewing beef, cut into 1-cm/½-in
    squares
3 tablespoons soy sauce
1 tablespoon sugar
1 tablespoon rice wine or sherry
½ teaspoon five-spice powder
450 g/1 lb carrots, cut diagonally into
    diamond shapes

MANGE-TOUT PEAS AND BEEF

SERVES 4

225 g/8 oz rump steak, thinly sliced
2 tablespoons oyster sauce
1 tablespoon rice wine or sherry
1 teaspoon cornflour
4 tablespoons oil
2 spring onions, cut into 2.5-cm/1-in lengths
1 slice fresh root ginger, peeled and cut
into strips
225 g/8 oz mange-tout peas, trimmed
1 tablespoon salt
1 teaspoon sugar

Cut the beef slices into narrow strips and put in a bowl with the oyster sauce, wine and cornflour. Mix well, then leave to marinate for about 20 minutes.

Heat 2 tablespoons of the oil in a wok and stir-fry the spring onions and ginger for a few seconds. Add the beef and stir-fry until evenly browned. Transfer the mixture to a warmed serving dish and keep hot.

Heat the remaining oil in the wok and stir-fry the mange-tout peas, salt and sugar for about 2 minutes. (Do not overcook, or the mange-tout peas will lose their texture and colour.) Add the mange-tout peas to the beef and mix well. Serve hot.

CURRY SAUCE

(not illustrated)

SERVES 4

4 tablespoons ghee or butter
1 large onion, sliced
2 cloves garlic, sliced
1 teaspoon ground coriander
1 teaspoon turmeric
1 teaspoon chilli powder
½ teaspoon salt
1 teaspoon freshly ground black pepper
300 ml/½ pint cold water
1 teaspoon garam masala

Melt the ghee in a wok, add the onion and garlic and fry gently until soft but not brown. Stir in the coriander, turmeric, chilli, salt and pepper. Fry for 5 minutes, then add the water and bring to the boil. Lower the heat and simmer for 10 minutes, then add the garam masala and simmer for a further 5 minutes.

Heat the oil in a wok and stir-fry the garlic, ginger and spring onion until golden brown. Add the beef, soy sauce, sugar, wine and five-spice powder.

Add just enough cold water to cover. Bring to the boil, lower the heat, cover and simmer for about 1½ hours.

Add the carrots to the beef and simmer for a further 30 minutes, or until tender. Serve hot.

Clockwise from bottom left: Stir-fried Beef with Broccoli; Beef and Carrot Stew; Mange-tout Peas and Beef

BEEF WITH GREEN PEPPER

SERVES 4

2–3 tablespoons oil
450 g/1 lb braising steak, cut into narrow
    strips, about 5-cm/2-in long
1 medium onion, chopped
50 g/2 oz raisins
1 large green pepper, seeded and cut
    into strips
50 g/2 oz desiccated coconut
1 teaspoon chilli powder
1 teaspoon garam masala
1 teaspoon ground cinnamon
1 teaspoon salt

Heat the oil in a wok and stir-fry the beef, onion
and raisins for about 5 minutes. Cover and cook
gently for about 45 minutes until the meat is
tender and there is no liquid left in the wok.

Add the green pepper, coconut, chilli powder,
garam masala, cinnamon and salt and stir-fry for a
further 2–3 minutes. (The finished dish should be
dry and the pepper crunchy.) Serve with dal and a
vegetable curry.

AFRICAN BEEF IN PEANUT SAUCE

SERVES 4

50 ml/2 fl oz oil
450 g/1 lb braising steak, cut into
    2.5-cm/1-in cubes
1 medium onion, roughly chopped
300 ml/$\frac{1}{2}$ pint water
100 g/4 oz fresh, unroasted peanuts, finely
    ground
2 tomatoes, skinned and roughly chopped
1 teaspoon chilli powder
1 teaspoon turmeric
salt

Heat the oil in a wok and stir-fry the beef and
onion for 5 minutes. Add the water, peanuts,
tomatoes, chilli powder, turmeric and salt and mix
thoroughly over a medium heat.

Bring to the boil, stirring occasionally. Cover,
reduce the heat and simmer for about 45 minutes
until the meat is tender. Remove the lid for the last
10 minutes and continue cooking until the sauce
has thickened.

BEEF WITH RUNNER BEANS

SERVES 4

2–3 tablespoons oil
1 large onion, finely chopped
2 cloves garlic, crushed
1 tablespoon ground coriander
1 tablespoon garam masala
1 teaspoon chilli powder
1 teaspoon sugar
450 g/1 lb braising steak, cut into
   2.5-cm/1-in cubes
1 (400-g/14-oz) can tomatoes, chopped with
   the juice
150 ml/$\frac{1}{4}$ pint water
salt
225 g/8 oz runner beans, trimmed and sliced
   diagonally into 2.5-cm/1-in lengths

Heat the oil in a wok and fry the onion until golden brown. Add the garlic and fry for a few seconds, then add the coriander, garam masala, chilli powder and sugar, and stir-fry for 1 minute.

Add the beef and seal on all sides, then stir in the tomatoes, water and salt. Reduce the heat, cover and cook for 1–1$\frac{1}{2}$ hours until the meat is tender and only a little liquid remains in the wok.

Add the runner beans, stir well and cook gently until the beans are tender and most of the liquid has evaporated.

MEATBALL CURRY

SERVES 4

675 g/1$\frac{1}{2}$ lb minced beef
2 cloves garlic, crushed
1 teaspoon salt
1 green chilli, seeded and finely chopped
1 quantity Curry Sauce (page 39)
300 ml/$\frac{1}{2}$ pint water
sprigs of fresh coriander to garnish

Place the beef, garlic, salt and chilli in a bowl and mix in well using a kneading action. Divide the mixture into 16 equal portions and, using a few drops of oil on the hands, roll each one into a smooth ball.

Place the curry sauce and water in a wok and bring to the boil. Lower the heat and simmer gently for a few minutes.

Lower the meatballs into the simmering sauce, stirring gently to ensure they are coated with the sauce. Cover and cook for 25–30 minutes.

Serve the meatball curry on a bed of plain boiled rice and garnish with coriander sprigs.

MINCED BEEF WITH AUBERGINE

SERVES 4

450 g/1 lb minced beef
1 large onion, chopped
2 cloves garlic, crushed
1 medium aubergine, cut into 5-cm/2-in
   lengths, 1-cm/½-in wide
1 tablespoon ground coriander
1 teaspoon ground ginger
2 teaspoons garam masala
1 (400-g/14-oz) can tomatoes, chopped with
   the juice
1 teaspoon chilli powder
1 teaspoon sugar
salt

Place the beef, onion and garlic in a wok over a
medium heat. Stir-fry until the fat is released from
the meat.

Add the aubergine, coriander, ginger and
garam masala and stir-fry for a further few
minutes. Stir in the tomatoes, chilli, sugar and salt.

Cover and cook gently for 25–30 minutes.
Transfer to a warmed serving dish and accompany
with rice.

MIDDLE-EASTERN MINCE

SERVES 4

Okra, native to Africa and known in the Middle
East as *bamia*, is now widely available in this
country. The ridged green pods are at their best
when they are fairly small and tender; avoid the
large pods which may be tough and stringy. It is
important not to overcook okra as the pods have a
tendency to become slimy. In this dish, lamb is
very lightly spiced with coriander and nutmeg
and cooked with tomatoes, then the whole okra
pods are added for a few minutes before the lamb is
served. A mixture of chick peas and sesame seeds
and a bowl of yogurt accompany the dish.

225 g/8 oz dried chick peas
salt and freshly ground black pepper
225 g/8 oz small okra
1 red pepper
1 green pepper
1 large onion, chopped
2 tablespoons oil
1 large clove garlic, crushed
450 g/1 lb minced lamb
1 teaspoon ground coriander
1 teaspoon freshly grated nutmeg
2 (400-g/14-oz) cans chopped tomatoes
1 tablespoon chopped fresh mint
grated rind and juice of ½ lemon
2 tablespoons sesame seeds
25 g/1 oz butter
150 ml/¼ pint natural yogurt to serve
   (optional)

Soak the chick peas overnight in plenty of cold
water. Next day, drain them and cook them in
plenty of boiling, lightly salted water for about 45
minutes, or until just tender.

Trim the stalks off the okra, then wipe each pod
with a damp cloth. Cut the peppers in half,
remove stalks, seeds and pith, chop the flesh and
mix with the onion. Heat the oil in a wok. Add the
garlic, peppers and onion and cook until the onion
is soft but not browned.

Add the lamb to the wok and fry it until it is
lightly browned, breaking it up with a wooden
spoon as it cooks. Stir in the coriander and nutmeg
and plenty of seasoning, then pour in the canned
tomatoes. Bring to the boil, cover the wok and
simmer gently for 20 minutes. Add the okra to the
meat mixture, stir well and re-cover the wok, then
continue to cook for a further 10 minutes, keeping
the mixture just simmering all the time. If the

can be used in place of fresh, in which case, allow it to defrost completely and remove any excess liquid by draining thoroughly.

2–3 tablespoons oil
1 large onion, finely chopped
2 cloves garlic, crushed
450 g/1 lb braising steak, cut into narrow strips
1 tablespoon ground coriander
1 teaspoon garam masala
1 teaspoon chilli powder
1 teaspoon mustard powder
salt
1 (225-g/8-oz) can tomatoes, chopped with the juice
225 g/8 oz broccoli, divided into florets

Heat the oil in a wok and fry the onion until lightly browned. Add the garlic and fry for a further minute.

Add the strips of beef and fry until sealed on all sides. Reduce the heat, cover and cook the meat in its own juices for about 45 minutes until tender.

Add the coriander, garam masala, chilli, mustard and salt and stir-fry over a low heat for a few seconds. Stir in the tomatoes and cook uncovered until almost dry.

Add the broccoli and stir-fry for a few minutes. Partly cover the wok and simmer until tender.

mixture is cooking too rapidly, then the okra will be overcooked.

Strain the cooked chick peas and sprinkle the mint, lemon rind and juice and sesame seeds over them. Add the butter and toss well to mix the ingredients. Spread the chick peas in a large warmed serving dish.

Pour the yogurt into a small dish to serve with the lamb. Ladle the lamb over the chick peas, then serve at once, with the yogurt and warmed pitta bread.

BEEF AND BROCCOLI CURRY

SERVES 4

The broccoli florets for this medium curry are used to add contrasting texture and colour. They should have tight, firm heads. Avoid those about to flower, as they break up easily and will disintegrate during the cooking. Frozen broccoli

LAMB AND LEEK CURRY

SERVES 4–6

50 ml/2 fl oz oil
675 g/1½ lb lamb, cut into 2.5-cm/1-in cubes
1 large onion, finely chopped
2 cloves garlic, crushed
50 g/2 oz fresh root ginger, chopped
150 ml/¼ pint natural yogurt
1 tablespoon plain flour
1 (225-g/8-oz) can tomatoes, chopped with
   the juice
1 tablespoon garam masala
1 teaspoon chilli powder
2 teaspoons sugar
2 teaspoons salt
150 ml/¼ pint water
450 g/1 lb leeks, trimmed, washed and cut
   into 2.5-cm/1-in pieces

Heat the oil in a wok and stir-fry the lamb, onion, garlic and ginger for 5 minutes. Add the remaining ingredients, except the leeks, and mix well.

Cover and cook gently for about 40 minutes, or until the lamb is tender.

Add the leeks to the wok and gently stir to cover the leeks with the sauce. Cook for a further 30 minutes, skimming off any excess fat if necessary. Serve with saffron rice and a side salad.

SESAME LAMB WITH SPINACH

SERVES 4–6

2–3 tablespoons oil
2 large onions, chopped
175 g/6 oz sesame seeds, ground
1 tablespoon ground coriander
1 tablespoon garam masala
1 teaspoon chilli powder
1 (75-g/3-oz) can tomato purée
300 ml/½ pint water
675 g/1½ lb lean lamb, cut into cubes
1 (450-g/1-lb) packet frozen spinach,
   thawed and chopped
2 teaspoons salt
1 teaspoon sugar

Heat the oil in a wok and fry the onions until just soft and transparent. Stir in the sesame seeds and fry gently for 2–3 minutes, stirring constantly to prevent burning.

Add the coriander, garam masala and chilli powder and fry for 5–8 seconds, then add the remaining ingredients and stir well.

Cover and cook gently for about 1 hour until the lamb is tender.

AFRICAN LAMB KARANGA

SERVES 4–6

2–3 tablespoons oil
1 large onion, finely chopped
1 teaspoon cumin seeds, crushed
100 g/4 oz fresh, unroasted peanuts,
   finely ground
1 tablespoon ground coriander
1 teaspoon chilli powder
1 (225-g/8-oz) can tomatoes, chopped with
   the juice
1 teaspoon salt
675 g/1½ lb lean lamb, cut into
   2.5-cm/1-in cubes
300 ml/½ pint water
150 ml/¼ pint soured cream to serve

Heat the oil in a wok and fry the onion until brown. Add the cumin seeds and peanuts and fry for 2–3 minutes, then add the coriander and chilli powder and fry for a few seconds.

Stir in the tomatoes and salt and fry for 4–5 minutes. Add the lamb and toss thoroughly in the mixture. Blend in the water.

Cover and cook gently for about 1 hour until the lamb is tender.

Serve on a bed of rice with swirls of soured cream on top, accompanied by a selection of pickles and chutneys.

Clockwise from top left: Sesame Lamb with Spinach; Lamb and Leek Curry; Lamb Karanga

Rice and Noodles

CHINESE FRIED RICE

SERVES 4–6

The Chinese mushrooms and sausages are available in Chinese stores and give an authentic flavour to this recipe. There are two kinds of soy sauce: one is dark and thick, like treacle, but the recipe uses the thin light soy sauce.

450 g/1 lb cold cooked rice
   (about 175 g/6 oz uncooked)
salt and freshly ground black pepper
6–8 tablespoons oil
1 egg, beaten
8 shallots or 2 small onions, sliced
3 cloves garlic, crushed
100 g/4 oz cooked, peeled prawns, thawed if
   frozen
100 g/4 oz Chinese sausage, sliced (optional)
100 g/4 oz cold roast pork, shredded
   (optional)
4 dried Chinese mushrooms, soaked in warm
   water for 30 minutes, drained and sliced
   (optional)
1–2 tablespoons light soy sauce
100 g/4 oz frozen peas, thawed
2 spring onions, sliced
1 red chilli, seeded and chopped (optional)
fresh coriander leaves (optional)

Garnish
shredded lettuce leaves
bay leaves (optional)

Cook the rice in a pan of boiling salted water until tender. Drain and leave until cold or cool overnight.

Heat a little of the oil in a frying pan and cook the egg to make an omelette. Roll up into a sausage and cut into fine strips. Reserve.

Heat 2 tablespoons of the oil in a wok and stir-fry the shallots or onions until crisp and golden brown. Lift out of the wok and reserve.

Add the garlic and prawns to the wok and cook for 1 minute, then set aside. Fry the Chinese sausage, shredded pork and mushrooms in the wok, then remove.

Heat sufficient oil in the wok to coat the rice completely. Stir-fry the rice for 2–3 minutes. Add the soy sauce, salt and pepper, plus half of the reserved cooked ingredients. Mix well. Add the peas and half the spring onions. Heat through for 3–4 minutes.

Serve the fried rice on a warmed serving platter and sprinkle with the remaining cooked ingredients, spring onion, the chilli and coriander leaves, if using. Surround the rice with a garnish of shredded lettuce and bay leaves, if liked.

NOODLES WITH MEAT AND VEGETABLES

SERVES 4–6

Similar to Chinese chow mein, this dish can be prepared with meat and seafood of your choice.

225 g/8 oz noodles
4 tablespoons oil
1 clove garlic, crushed
225 g/8 oz boned lean pork, thinly sliced
225 g/8 oz chicken breast meat, thinly sliced
225 g/8 oz cooked, peeled prawns, deveined
and diced
1 medium onion, thinly sliced
100 g/4 oz shredded cabbage
2 tablespoons fish sauce
175 ml/6 fl oz chicken stock
pinch of paprika
$\frac{1}{2}$ teaspoon salt
freshly ground black pepper

Garnish
2 hard-boiled eggs, quartered
2 spring onions, chopped
few lemon wedges

Cook the noodles in a pan of boiling water for about 2 minutes until slightly undercooked. Drain, rinse under cold running water, then drain again. Place in a bowl with 1 tablespoon of the oil and mix.

Heat 1 tablespoon of the oil in a wok. Add the noodles and fry until golden brown on all sides, then remove from the wok.

Wipe the wok clean with absorbent kitchen paper, then add 1 tablespoon of the oil and the garlic. Fry until the garlic is brown, then add the pork and fry for 5 minutes. Add the chicken and prawns and stir-fry for 2 minutes over high heat. Remove all the ingredients from the wok.

Wipe the wok clean again with absorbent kitchen paper and place over high heat. When it is very hot, add the remaining oil, then the onion and cabbage. Stir-fry for about 4 minutes until the onion is translucent but the cabbage is still undercooked and crunchy.

Add the remaining ingredients, stir well, then add the cooked meat and fish mixture. Heat through for 2 minutes until most of the juices have evaporated, stirring constantly.

Add the noodles to the wok, toss well and cook until heated through. Pile on to a warmed serving dish. Garnish with the eggs, spring onions and lemon wedges. Serve hot.

FRIED RICE WITH PORK AND PRAWNS

SERVES 4

Oriental-style fried rice makes a good supper dish. Serve the rice straight from the wok or in one big serving bowl with small bowls and chopsticks for each person so that everyone dips into the pan of rice to take what they require. If you want to make the dish really economical, then omit the prawns and use button mushrooms instead of the Chinese dried mushrooms.

4 dried Chinese mushrooms
4 tablespoons oil
a few drops of sesame oil
1 clove garlic, crushed
225 g/8 oz long-grain rice
450 g/1 lb minced pork
1 (227-g/8-oz) can water chestnuts, drained
  and sliced
4 tablespoons soy sauce
450 ml/$\frac{3}{4}$ pint water
2 eggs, beaten
225 g/8 oz peeled cooked prawns
4 spring onions, shredded

Put the mushrooms in a small basin and pour in enough hot water to cover them. Put a saucer on top to keep them in the water and leave them to soak for 30 minutes.

Meanwhile, heat 3 tablespoons of the oil in a wok, add the sesame oil and garlic, then stir in the rice and stir-fry until the grains are transparent. Add the pork and continue to cook, stirring frequently, until the meat is lightly cooked.

While the pork is cooking, drain the mushrooms and slice them thinly. Add them to the wok with the water chestnuts and pour in the soy sauce. Stir in the water, then bring to the boil. Reduce the heat and cover the wok tightly, then leave to simmer for 10 minutes.

Meanwhile heat the remaining 1 tablespoon oil in a large frying pan until really hot, then pour in the beaten eggs and cook quickly until they are bubbling and begin to set. Lift the sides of this omelette to allow any uncooked egg to run on to the pan. When the omelette has completely set and the underneath is well browned, use a large fish slice to turn it over. If you are not confident that you can do this, invert it on to a large plate and then slide it back into the pan. When cooked, slide the omelette out on to a plate lined with absorbent kitchen paper.

Add the prawns to the rice mixture but do not stir them in. Replace the lid on the pan and cook for a further 10 minutes. Cut the omelette first into thin strips, then across into 2.5-cm/1-in lengths. When the rice is cooked, fork the prawns, omelette pieces and spring onions into the grains and serve at once.

PORK PEARLS

SERVES 4

These are steamed meatballs which are coated in rice. The uncooked grains of rice cling to the raw meat and as the meatballs are steamed, the grains cook and expand. Serve the pork pearls with some mixed stir-fried vegetables – Chinese cabbage, beansprouts, spring onions, sliced water chestnuts and bamboo shoots – to make a light main course.

450 g/1 lb minced pork
$\frac{1}{2}$ teaspoon five-spice powder
2 tablespoons soy sauce
a few drops of sesame oil
1 egg, beaten
2 tablespoons dry sherry
225 g/8 oz long-grain rice (not easy-cook)
1 small cucumber to garnish

Mix the pork with the five-spice powder, soy sauce, sesame oil and egg. Add the sherry and stir thoroughly to make sure that the spice is well mixed in. Take small spoonfuls of the mixture and shape each into a small ball about the size of a walnut – you should have 24 meatballs. Roll each meatball in the rice so that the grains stick to it. The wok makes a wonderful steamer, so arrange the meatballs on a heatproof plate and place on the steaming rack, cover and steam over boiling water for 45 minutes.

For the garnish, very lightly peel the cucumber (you should remove only the tough part of the skin and leave a bright green covering). Trim the ends off, cut the cucumber into 7.5-cm/3-in lengths and slice each piece lengthways. Put the slices in a bowl with enough cold water to cover them and add some ice cubes. Leave for at least 30 minutes.

To serve, thoroughly drain the cucumber, then toss the pieces together and arrange them on the edge of a large platter. Pile the pork pearls in the middle and serve.

Top left: Pork Pearls; *bottom left*: Fried Rice with Pork and Prawns; *below*: 'Ants climbing Trees'

'ANTS CLIMBING TREES'

SERVES 3–4

This strangely named dish is quite simply stir-fried minced pork mixed with cellophane noodles.

225 g/8 oz boned pork, minced
2 tablespoons soy sauce
1 tablespoon sugar
1 teaspoon cornflour
½ teaspoon chilli sauce
3 tablespoons oil
1 small red chilli, seeded and chopped
2 spring onions, chopped
75 g/3 oz cellophane noodles, soaked in water
  for 30 minutes
120 ml/4 fl oz chicken stock or water
shredded spring onion to garnish

Put the pork in a bowl with the soy sauce, sugar, cornflour and chilli sauce. Mix well, then leave to marinate for about 20 minutes.

Heat the oil in a wok and stir-fry the chilli and spring onions for a few seconds, then add the pork. Stir-fry until the pork changes colour.

Drain the noodles, then add to the wok. Blend well. Add the stock or water and continue cooking until all the liquid has been absorbed. Serve hot, garnished with shredded spring onion.

Vegetable Dishes

TANGY POTATOES WITH PEAS

(not illustrated)

SERVES 4

This recipe is similar to the one which follows but more highly flavoured and the vegetables are coated with a thick tomato sauce.

50 ml/2 fl oz oil
½ teaspoon fenugreek seeds
1 teaspoon black mustard seeds
4 medium potatoes, peeled and cut into
   2.5-cm/1-in cubes
225 g/8 oz fresh or frozen peas
1 tablespoon ground coriander
1 teaspoon turmeric
1 teaspoon chilli powder
1 (225-g/8-oz) can tomatoes, chopped with
   the juice
salt
1 teaspoon sugar

Heat the oil in a wok and fry the fenugreek seeds until browned. Add the mustard seeds and fry until they pop.

Reduce the heat, then add the potatoes and peas and cover to preserve the flavour. Cook for 5 minutes.

Uncover and add the coriander, turmeric, chilli powder, tomatoes, salt and sugar. Cover and cook for about 30 minutes, stirring occasionally, until the vegetables are tender and most of the liquid has reduced to a thickened sauce.

SPICY PEAS AND POTATOES

SERVES 4

2 tablespoons oil
225 g/8 oz fresh or frozen peas
225 g/8 oz potatoes, peeled and diced
225 g/8 oz onions, diced
1 tablespoon garam masala
1 teaspoon turmeric
1 teaspoon chilli powder

Heat the oil in a wok and stir-fry the peas, potatoes, onions, garam masala, turmeric and chilli powder for a few minutes to mix well.

Cover and cook gently for about 25–30 minutes or until the vegetables are tender. Stir occasionally during the cooking time to prevent sticking. Serve as an accompaniment to meat.

RUNNER BEAN CURRY

SERVES 4–6

50 ml/2 fl oz oil
1 teaspoon black mustard seeds
675 g/1½ lb runner beans, trimmed and sliced
   diagonally in 2-cm/¾-in slices
1 medium onion, sliced
1 tablespoon ground coriander
1 teaspoon garam masala
1 teaspoon chilli powder
1 (225-g/8-oz) can tomatoes, chopped with
   the juice
salt

Heat the oil in a wok and fry the mustard seeds until they pop. Reduce the heat and stir-fry the runner beans and onion for 2 minutes.

Add the ground coriander, garam masala and chilli powder and mix well. Stir in the tomatoes and salt.

Cover and cook gently for about 20 minutes until the vegetables are tender. Stir occasionally during the cooking time to prevent sticking.

FRENCH BEANS WITH POTATOES

SERVES 4–6

3–4 tablespoons oil
1 medium onion, sliced
4 medium potatoes, peeled and cut into
    2.5-cm/1-in cubes
450 g/1 lb fresh or frozen green beans, sliced
1 teaspoon ground mixed spice
1 teaspoon ground cinnamon
1 teaspoon turmeric
1 teaspoon cumin seeds, crushed
salt

Heat the oil in a wok and stir-fry the onion, potatoes, green beans, mixed spice, cinnamon, turmeric, cumin and salt for 2–3 minutes.

Cover and cook gently for about 25 minutes until the vegetables are tender. (If using fresh beans, it may be necessary to add 2–3 tablespoons water.)

Clockwise from top right: French Beans with Potatoes; Runner Bean Curry; Spicy Peas and Potatoes

MILD POTATO AND ONION CURRY

SERVES 4–6

50 ml/2 fl oz oil
1 teaspoon black mustard seeds
675 g/1½ lb potatoes, peeled and cubed
1 large onion, sliced
1 teaspoon ground coriander
1 teaspoon chilli powder
1 teaspoon turmeric
salt
600 ml/1 pint water

Heat the oil in a wok and fry the mustard seeds until they pop. Reduce the heat and add the potatoes, onion, coriander, chilli powder, turmeric and salt. Toss the ingredients to mix well.

Add the water gradually, stirring carefully. Increase the heat slightly, then cover and cook for about 25 minutes until the potatoes are just tender.

Before serving, lift out a few pieces of potato and mash them. Return the mashed potatoes to the wok and stir thoroughly to thicken the sauce. Serve with a dry meat or vegetable curry such as Beef with Green Pepper (page 40) or Stuffed Okra (page 60).

Clockwise from bottom left: Mild Potato and Onion Curry; Mildly Spiced Spinach and Aubergine; Aubergine and Peas

52

Heat the oil in a wok and fry the fenugreek seeds until browned. Add the mustard and cumin seeds and fry until they begin to pop.

Carefully add the peas and aubergine, reduce the heat, cover and fry for a few seconds. Add the coriander, chilli powder, turmeric and salt, and stir well. Add the tomatoes and water and mix thoroughly.

Cover and cook for about 30 minutes, stirring once or twice during the cooking time.

A few minutes before serving, add the chopped coriander, stir and complete the cooking time. Serve with a meat or chicken curry of your choice.

MILDLY SPICED SPINACH AND AUBERGINE

SERVES 4

1 large aubergine
50 ml/2 fl oz oil
1 teaspoon fenugreek seeds
1 (450-g/1-lb) packet frozen spinach, thawed
  and chopped
1 medium onion, sliced
1 tablespoon ground coriander
1 teaspoon turmeric
salt

Cut the aubergine into strips, 5 × 2.5-cm/2 × 1-in. Reserve in a bowl of cold water to prevent discolouring. Before using, drain and dry on absorbent kitchen paper.

Heat the oil in a wok and fry the fenugreek seeds until browned. Reduce the heat and carefully add the aubergine, spinach, onion, coriander, turmeric and salt, stirring well.

Cover and cook the vegetables in their own juices for about 30 minutes or until tender.

AUBERGINE AND PEAS

SERVES 4–6

50 ml/2 fl oz oil
1 teaspoon fenugreek seeds
1 teaspoon black mustard seeds
1 teaspoon cumin seeds
450 g/1 lb fresh or frozen peas
1 medium aubergine, about 175 g–225 g/
  6–8 oz, cut into cubes
1 tablespoon ground coriander
1 teaspoon chilli powder
1 teaspoon turmeric
salt
1 (225-g/8-oz) can tomatoes, chopped with
  the juice
50 ml/2 fl oz water
5–6 sprigs of fresh coriander, chopped

SWEET AND SOUR POTATO CURRY

SERVES 4–6

50 ml/2 fl oz oil
1 teaspoon black mustard seeds
1 teaspoon cumin seeds
6 medium potatoes, peeled and cubed
2 teaspoons ground coriander
1 teaspoon turmeric
1 teaspoon chilli powder
2 teaspoons salt
4 teaspoons brown sugar
300 ml/½ pint water
1 (75-g/3-oz) can tomato purée
3 tablespoons vinegar
5–6 sprigs of fresh coriander, chopped, to
    garnish

Heat the oil in a wok and fry the mustard and cumin seeds together until they pop. Reduce the heat and carefully add the potatoes. Add the remaining ingredients and stir well.

Cover and cook gently for about 30 minutes until the potatoes are tender, and a large amount of thick sauce remains in the wok. Serve garnished with the chopped coriander.

POTATOES AND AUBERGINE WITH PEANUTS

SERVES 4–6

120 ml/4 fl oz oil
2 teaspoons cumin seeds
100 g/4 oz fresh, unroasted peanuts, ground
1 medium onion, chopped
6 medium potatoes, peeled and cut into
    2.5-cm/1-in cubes
1 large aubergine, cut into 2.5-cm/1-in cubes
1 (400-g/14-oz) can tomatoes, chopped with
    the juice
300 ml/½ pint water
1 tablespoon ground coriander
1 teaspoon garam masala
1 teaspoon chilli powder
1 teaspoon turmeric
2 teaspoons salt

Heat the oil in a wok and fry the cumin seeds until they pop. Add the ground peanuts and fry for 1 minute only.

Reduce the heat, add the onion and fry for a further minute. Add the potatoes and aubergine and stir-fry for a few seconds. Add the remaining ingredients, stirring well.

Cover and cook gently for about 25–30 minutes. Stir occasionally during the cooking time to prevent sticking. Serve with chapatis or naan bread.

SPINACH AND ONION CURRY

SERVES 4

This medium vegetable curry makes a delicious accompanying dish with any meal in summer, when fresh spinach is plentiful. If using frozen spinach, it will be easier to chop when only partially thawed, but allow to thaw completely before using.

50 ml/2 fl oz oil
1 teaspoon fenugreek seeds
1 (450-g/1-lb) packet frozen spinach, thawed
    and chopped
225 g/8 oz onions, sliced
1 tablespoon ground coriander
1 teaspoon garam masala
1 teaspoon chilli powder
1 teaspoon turmeric
salt

Heat the oil in a wok and fry the fenugreek seeds until browned. Reduce the heat and carefully add the spinach, then the onions, coriander, garam masala, chilli powder, turmeric and salt. Mix thoroughly.

Cover and cook the vegetables in their own juices for about 20–25 minutes.

From the top: Sweet and Sour Potato Curry; Potatoes and Aubergine with Peanuts; Spinach and Onion Curry

SWEETCORN CURRY

SERVES 4

Kassaro is the Swahili name for sweetcorn in Uganda. However, in Kenya it is known as Mahindi meaning Indian. The Indian traders made sweetcorn popular in the very early 1900s as they came down to settle in the East African coast.

2–3 tablespoons oil
1 tablespoon cumin seeds
1 (450-g/1-lb) packet frozen sweetcorn
 kernels
1 teaspoon ground coriander
1 teaspoon garam masala
5–6 sprigs of fresh coriander, chopped
salt
4 tomatoes, chopped
tomato slices to garnish

Heat the oil in a wok and fry the cumin seeds until they crackle. Add the sweetcorn, ground coriander, garam masala, chopped fresh coriander, salt and tomatoes and stir well.

Cover and cook gently for about 20–25 minutes. Serve garnished with slices of tomato.

Variation
Two (425-g/14½-oz) cans sweetcorn kernels, drained, may be used in place of the frozen sweetcorn. After the cumin seeds have been fried, all the ingredients can be stir-fried together until heated through.

SPICY CAULIFLOWER

SERVES 4

50 ml/2 fl oz oil
1 tablespoon cumin seeds
1 medium onion, sliced
450 g/1 lb cauliflower, divided into florets
100 g/4 oz fresh or frozen peas
100 g/4 oz carrots, cut into strips about
 5-cm/2-in long
1 tablespoon ground coriander
1 teaspoon turmeric
1 teaspoon chilli powder
salt
5–6 sprigs of fresh coriander, chopped

Heat the oil in a wok and fry the cumin seeds until they crackle. Add the onion and fry quickly until lightly browned.

Reduce the heat and add the cauliflower, peas, carrots, coriander, turmeric, chilli powder and salt. Stir well.

Cover and cook the vegetables in their own juices over a low heat for about 30 minutes until tender and most of the liquid has evaporated.

A few minutes before serving, sprinkle the chopped coriander over the vegetables. Cook, uncovered, for a further 5 minutes, tossing frequently. Serve immediately with chapatis, plain boiled rice and natural yogurt.

Clockwise from left: Spicy Cauliflower; Sweetcorn Curry; Spicy Fried Courgettes

SPICY FRIED COURGETTES

SERVES 4

2–3 tablespoons oil
1 medium onion, finely chopped
6–8 medium courgettes, cut into 1-cm/½-in
   slices
1 tablespoon cumin seeds, finely ground
½ teaspoon grated nutmeg
1 teaspoon chilli powder
1 teaspoon turmeric
salt

Heat the oil in a wok and stir-fry the onion and courgettes for 10 minutes.

Add the cumin seeds, nutmeg, chilli powder, turmeric and salt and stir-fry for a further 5–10 minutes.

Serve either as a starter on their own or with a dry fish dish.

Note: Choose even-sized courgettes which are about 10–15-cm/4–6-in long so that they all cook at the same time.

CURRIED OKRA AND POTATOES

SERVES 4

450 g/1 lb okra, trimmed
4 tablespoons oil
1 teaspoon black mustard seeds
1 medium onion, sliced lengthways
225 g/8 oz potatoes, peeled and cut into
    2.5-cm/1-in cubes
1 teaspoon salt
1 teaspoon turmeric
1 teaspoon chilli powder
1 tablespoon ground coriander
2 tomatoes, chopped
4 sprigs of fresh coriander, chopped, to
    garnish

Cut each okra in half, then cut each half into 4 lengthways and reserve.

Heat the oil in a wok and fry the mustard seeds until they begin to pop. Add the onion and stir-fry for 2–3 minutes.

Reduce the heat and carefully add the okra and potatoes, then the salt, turmeric, chilli powder and ground coriander. Toss the ingredients well. Cover and cook for about 25 minutes, tossing the vegetables every few minutes.

Stir in the chopped tomatoes, toss well and cook for a further 10–15 minutes. Serve sprinkled with chopped fresh coriander.

SPICED OKRA

SERVES 4

450 g/1 lb okra, trimmed
50 ml/2 fl oz oil
1 teaspoon fenugreek seeds
1 tablespoon ground coriander
1 teaspoon turmeric
1 teaspoon chilli powder
salt
5–6 sprigs of fresh coriander, chopped, to
    garnish

Cut the okra into 2.5-cm/1-in rings.

Heat the oil in a wok and fry the fenugreek seeds until browned. Add the okra, ground coriander, turmeric, chilli powder and salt and toss to mix thoroughly.

Cook, uncovered, over a low heat for about 20 minutes, tossing frequently until the okra is tender and dry. Serve sprinkled with fresh coriander.

OKRA WITH TOMATOES

(not illustrated)

SERVES 4

Serve this lighly spiced vegetable mixture as an accompaniment to curries, or with simple grilled, fried or barbecued meats.

450 g/1 lb okra
450 g/1 lb tomatoes
1 small onion
25 g/1 oz butter
2 tablespoons oil
4 green cardamoms
salt and freshly ground black pepper
1 teaspoon garam masala
2 tablespoons chopped fresh coriander leaves

Trim off and discard the ends of the okra and slice them into chunks. Place the tomatoes in a large bowl and pour in enough boiling water to cover them. Allow to stand for 30 seconds to a minute, then drain and peel them. Thinly slice the onion and quarter the peeled tomatoes.

Melt the butter and oil in the wok and add the cardamoms. Fry these for a few seconds, then add the onion and a little salt and pepper and cook until soft but not browned. Add the okra and tomatoes and cook for a few minutes, stirring the vegetables frequently. The okra should be tender but take care not to overcook them because then they become slimy and unpleasant in texture.

As soon as the vegetables are cooked, sprinkle on the garam masala and chopped coriander and serve immediately.

Note: When preparing okra, it is important to remember that they should never be washed under running water before cooking, as this makes them slimy. Simply wipe them with a damp cloth or with moistened absorbent kitchen paper. Discard any that are damaged.

Top: Spiced Okra; *bottom:* Curried Okra and Potatoes

STUFFED OKRA

SERVES 4

A dry curry originating from Gujarat in India. The stuffing varies from district to district. It is essential to use young, unblemished okra as they are cooked untrimmed.

450 g/1 lb young okra
75 ml/3 fl oz oil
1 medium onion, minced
1 tablespoon ground coriander
1 tablespoon garam masala
1 teaspoon chilli powder
1 teaspoon turmeric
1 teaspoon salt
1 tablespoon tomato purée
banana slices to garnish

Make a slit on one side of each okra to form a pocket.

Combine 2 tablespoons of the oil with the remaining ingredients in a bowl and mix well. Use the mixture to stuff each okra, pressing it well into the pocket.

Heat the remaining oil in a wok and gently lower the stuffed okra into the oil. Cook, uncovered, over a medium heat for about 25 minutes, tossing frequently to prevent sticking.

To serve, arrange the stuffed okra attractively on a warmed serving dish and garnish with sliced banana.

DRY CABBAGE AND CARROT CURRY

SERVES 6

75 ml/3 fl oz oil
1 tablespoon cumin seeds
450 g/1 lb white cabbage, finely shredded
225 g/8 oz carrots, diced
1 tablespoon ground coriander
1 teaspoon chilli powder
2 teaspoons salt
1 (225-g/8-oz) can tomatoes, chopped with the juice
5–6 sprigs of fresh coriander, chopped, to garnish

Heat the oil in a wok and fry the cumin seeds until they crackle. Add the cabbage and carrots, then reduce the heat and add the ground coriander, chilli powder and salt and mix well. Stir in the tomatoes.

Cover and cook over a low heat for about 30–45 minutes, stirring frequently, until almost dry. Sprinkle with fresh coriander and serve with saffron rice. This dry curry would go well with a lamb curry.

DRY MIXED VEGETABLE CURRY

SERVES 4

2–3 tablespoons oil
1 medium carrot, diced
1 medium onion, diced
1 medium potato, peeled and diced
1 small cauliflower, divided into florets
1 tablespoon ground coriander
1 tablespoon garam masala
1 teaspoon chilli powder
salt
5–6 sprigs of fresh coriander, coarsely chopped

Heat the oil in a wok and stir-fry the carrot, onion, potato and cauliflower for 2–3 minutes. Add the ground coriander, garam masala, chilli powder, salt and fresh coriander and stir well.

Cover and cook for 25–30 minutes until the vegetables are tender. Stir occasionally, making sure that each time the lid is lifted no water falls back into the vegetables – this ensures the dryness of the curry.

SPICY KALE AND POTATOES

SERVES 4

50 ml/2 fl oz oil
450 g/1 lb kale, shredded
225 g/8 oz potatoes, peeled and cut into 2.5-cm/1-in cubes
1 medium onion, sliced
1 tablespoon ground coriander
1 teaspoon turmeric
salt

Heat the oil in a wok and stir-fry the kale, potatoes, onion, coriander, turmeric and salt over a low heat for a few minutes to mix well.

Cover and cook in their own juices for about 25 minutes until the potatoes are tender and most of the liquid has evaporated.

Top: Dry Mixed Vegetable Curry; *bottom:* Spicy Kale and Potatoes

GLOSSARY

Bamboo shoot Bamboo shoots are sold fresh in Chinese supermarkets but are most commonly found canned in water or brine. The fresh shoots must be thickly peeled, then cooked in boiling water until tender. The canned shoots are quite acceptable and they can be stored in fresh water in a covered container in the refrigerator for 1–2 weeks. Change water daily.

Bean curd Also known as *tofu*, this white curd has a texture similar to a firmly set custard. Prepared from soya beans, the bean curd is bland and it readily absorbs the flavour of other foods; it is also highly nutritious. Sliced or cut into pieces the bean curd can be included in soups and stir-fries. Available from Chinese supermarkets, health food shops and some supermarkets.

Cardamoms, pods and seeds Cardamoms are white or green and have parchment-like skins and lots of tiny, round black, highly aromatic seeds inside. The pods are usually available in supermarkets. When used whole, cardamom pods are not meant to be eaten; if you like they can be removed before serving the dish.

When a recipe calls for cardamom seeds, carefully remove the seeds from the pods. Alternatively you can buy the seeds from the few Indian and Pakistani grocers who sell them.

Cellophane noodles, Bean thread or Mung bean thread These very fine, translucent dried noodles are made from mung bean flour. Available from oriental supermarkets, cellophane noodles are sold wrapped in bundles and need to be soaked in cold water for about 10 minutes before use.

Coconut, fresh grated When buying coconuts, make sure that they are crack-free and have no mould on them. Shake them to make sure that they are heavy with liquid. To remove the liquid, pierce two of the 'eyes' in the top of the coconut, then drain the juice into a jug. (The liquid is not used in cooking, but you may drink it.) Use a hammer to crack open the nut, then prise off the coconut flesh from the hard shell with a knife. Peel off the brown coconut skin with a potato peeler and break the flesh into 2.5-cm/1-in pieces (larger ones if you are grating manually). Wash these coconut pieces and either grate them finely on a hand grater or else put them in a liquidiser or food processor. Grated coconut freezes beautifully and defrosts fast.

Coconut milk Coconut milk is prepared from grated fresh coconut flesh which is soaked in water then squeezed out. The liquid is thick coconut milk; if the squeezed-out coconut is soaked again, then the second batch of liquid is thin coconut milk. Coconut milk is also sold canned, or in a concentrated form in small blocks to be dissolved in hot water. Desiccated coconut can also be soaked in hot water, then squeezed out to make coconut milk.

Coriander, fresh green A favourite Indian herb used both as a garnish and for its flavour. This pretty green plant resembles flat-leaf parsley and grows to about 15–20 cm/6–8 in. in height. Just the top leafy section is used, though the stems are sometimes thrown into pulse dishes for their aroma. This herb is worth hunting for as its delicate flavour is unique. It is sold by Asian grocers, some supermarkets, and market stalls, and can also be grown at home from coriander seeds.

Coriander seeds, whole and ground These are the round, beige seeds of the coriander plant. They are generally used in their ground form and may be bought ready-ground from supermarkets and ethnic grocers. You could also buy the whole seeds and grind them yourself in small quantities in an electric coffee-grinder or in a pestle and mortar.

Cumin seeds, whole and ground The whole seeds are sold by specialist grocers and by some supermarkets. The ground seeds can be found in nearly all supermarkets. Whole seeds keep their flavour much longer and may be ground very easily in an electric coffee-grinder. To roast cumin seeds put them into a small, heavy frying pan (cast-iron frying pans are best for this) without any fat and place the pan over a low heat. No fat is necessary. Stir the seeds and keep roasting them until they turn a few shades darker. The seeds emit a wonderful aroma when they are ready. When cool store the roasted seeds in an airtight container.

Fenugreek seeds The yellowish, dried seeds come from the pods of an Asian flowering plant and have a slightly bitter taste. Ground fenugreek seeds are commonly included in ready-made curry powders. Buy from Asian stores.

Fish sauce Known as *patis* in the Philippines, *nam pla* in Thailand, *nuoc cham* or *nuoc mam* in Kampuchea, Laos and Vietnam. Fish sauce is as important to these schools of cooking as salt is in the west. Prepared from fresh anchovies and salt which are layered in wooden barrels and left to ferment. Caramel, molasses, rice or boiled corn may be added as extra flavourings.

Five spice powder The five ground spices that compose this dark powder are star anise, anise pepper, fennel, cloves and cinnamon. Delicatessens and oriental stores stock it.

Garam masala A mixture of roasted spices, much used in Indian cooking. Buy ready-prepared or prepare your own mixture. Recipes vary, but the following is a good example of ingredients and proportions: $1\frac{1}{2}$ teaspoons cardamom pods, 5 teaspoons coriander seeds, 1 teaspoon cumin seeds, $1\frac{1}{2}$ teaspoons whole cloves, 6 teaspoons whole black peppercorns. The seeds are removed from the cardamoms, then all the spices are baked in a very hot oven for 10 minutes. Cool, then grind to a fine powder, using a pestle and mortar, and store in an airtight jar.

Ginger, fresh root The knobbly ginger root has a refreshing, pungent flavour and a smooth beige-brown coloured skin which varies slightly in thickness. Young root ginger has a light, thin skin and smooth quite juicy, tender flesh. The older more common ginger has a fairly thick skin and slightly fibrous flesh. The root should not be wrinkled even if it is older.

Available from greengrocers and supermarkets or Chinese and Indian shops, the ginger can be stored in a plastic bag in the refrigerator for several weeks (check to make sure that any cut ends do not develop a mould) or in a pot of sand. The root can be grated without being peeled or it can be peeled, then thinly sliced and cut into fine shreds. To grate ginger into a pulp, use the finest part of a hand grater. To grind ginger into a paste, chop it coarsely first and then process it in a food processor or liquidiser. Add just enough water to make as smooth a paste as possible.

Lemon Grass Fresh lemon grass is available from Oriental supermarkets. The lower third of the stalk, the bulb-like portion, is the part to use when a recipe specifies 'chopped or sliced lemon grass'. Alternatively the whole stalk (stem) may be bruised and added during cooking, but then it should be removed before serving. Dried lemon grass is a good substitute; soak in hot water for about 2 hours before using, then remove from the dish before serving.

Macadamia nuts Australian in origin, where they are also known as Queensland nuts, they are now grown in Hawaii as well. The flavour of the macadamia is buttery and sweet and the almond makes a suitable substitute if macadamias are unavailable. They are usually sold shelled and roasted.

Mushrooms, dried Chinese Available from oriental supermarkets, these large mushrooms have rough stems and must be soaked in water until soft; the stems can then be removed if they are still tough. The mushrooms have a distinctive flavour and a substantial texture, almost 'meaty'.

Mustard seeds, whole black These are round, tiny and not really black but a dark reddish-brown colour. When scattered into hot oil they turn deliciously nutty. Buy mustard seeds at Indian and Pakistani grocers.

Oyster sauce A concentrated sauce prepared from oysters, soy sauce and brine, this is a brown liquid which intensifies the flavour of other foods. Easily available in jars and bottles from good supermarkets, delicatessens and oriental shops.

Rice papers Thin, brittle, disc-like pancakes, rice papers are made from the pith of an oriental tree. They are used as a wrapper for a variety of foods and must be moistened with water or egg to make them flexible before using. Rice papers are most familiar in forming the base of macaroons and nougat and are readily available from supermarkets.

Rice wine This clear white wine is more closely related to spirit or fortified wine than to ordinary white wine as we know it. It is used to enhance pork and chicken flavours and to add fragrance to all sorts of dishes. Sherry is a good substitute if you do not live anywhere near a good oriental supermarket.

Shrimp paste Made from salted dried shrimps. Greyish pink in colour. It is available in jars from Chinese stores.

Soy sauce Made from fermented soya beans, this is an essential condiment in Chinese cookery, used as extensively as salt is in the west. Most commonly it is dark and pungently flavoured, but a more delicate – yet very salty – light soy sauce is also available from supermarkets, delicatessens and oriental stores.

Tamarind water Tamarind water is obtained from the dried pulp of the acid-flavoured tamarind fruit. The dried pulp is sold in blocks in oriental supermarkets. Soak about 25 g/1 oz tamarind pulp in 300 ml/½ pint water for 5–10 minutes, then squeeze, strain and use the sharply sour juice. The longer the tamarind is left to soak, the stronger the flavour.

Turmeric Turmeric is valued for its colour more than its flavour, although it has the qualities of being a digestive and an antiseptic. Use it carefully as it can stain. Depending on the other ingredients in a dish, it will turn curries ochre or clear yellow. Remember, it has quite a different flavour from saffron for which it is often substituted.

Water chestnuts A crunchy texture characterises these round white chestnuts, used sliced or chopped. They are stocked in cans by supermarkets as well as by specialist shops.

Wun tun skins Paper-thin squares or circles of dough. They can be made at home or bought ready-rolled and trimmed at Chinese supermarkets. Store in the refrigerator or freezer.

INDEX